DAVID WILLIAMSON's first full-length play, *The Coming of Stork*, premiered at the La Mama Theatre, Carlton, in 1970 and later became the film *Stork*, directed by Tim Burstall.

The Removalists and *Don's Party* followed in 1971, then *Jugglers Three* (1972), *What If You Died Tomorrow?* (1973), *The Department* (1975), *A Handful of Friends* (1976), *The Club* (1977) and *Travelling North* (1979). In 1972 *The Removalists* won the Australian Writers' Guild AWGIE Award for best stage play and the best script in any medium and the British production saw Williamson nominated most promising playwright by the London *Evening Standard*.

The 1980s saw his success continue with *Celluloid Heroes* (1980), *The Perfectionist* (1982), *Sons of Cain* (1985), *Emerald City* (1987) and *Top Silk* (1989); whilst the 1990s produced *Siren* (1990), *Money and Friends* (1991), *Brilliant Lies* (1993), *Sanctuary* (1994), *Dead White Males* (1995), *Heretic* (1996), *Third World Blues* (an adaptation of *Jugglers Three*) and *After the Ball* (both in 1997), and *Corporate Vibes* and *Face to Face* (both in 1999). *The Great Man* (2000), *Up for Grabs, A Conversation, Charitable Intent* (all in 2001), *Soulmates* (2002), *Birthrights* (2003), *Amigos, Flatfoot* (both in 2004), *Scarlett O'Hara at the Crimson Parrot* (2008), *Let the Sunshine* (2009), *Rhinestone Rex and Miss Monica* (2010) and *Don Parties On* (2011) have since followed.

Williamson is widely recognised as Australia's most successful playwright and over the last thirty years his plays have been performed throughout Australia and produced in Britain, United States, Canada and many European countries. A number of his stage works have been adapted for the screen, including *The Removalists, Don's Party, The Club, Travelling North, Emerald City, Sanctuary* and *Brilliant Lies*.

Williamson was the principal screenwriter for *Balibo* which won the 2010 Australian Film Institute Award for best adapted screenplay. He has also won the Australian Film Institute film script award for *Petersen* (1974), *Don's Party* (1976), *Gallipoli* (1981) and *Travelling North* (1987) and has won twelve Australian Writers' Guild AWGIE Awards. He lives on Queensland's Sunshine Coast with his writer wife, Kristin Williamson.

DON's PARTY

CURRENCY PRESS
SYDNEY

David Williamson

First published in 1973
by Currency Press Pty Ltd,
PO Box 2287, Strawberry Hills, NSW, 2012, Australia
enquiries@currency.com.au
www.currency.com.au

This revised edition published in 1997

Reprinted 2005 (twice), 2006, 2007, 2008, 2011

NATIONAL LIBRARY OF AUSTRALIA CIP DATA
    Williamson, David, 1972–
    Don's Party.
        ISBN 978 0 86819 530 8.
        1. Title
        A822.3

Cover design byEmma Vine, Currency Press.

Contents

Currency Press acknowledges the Traditional Owners of the Country on which
we live and work. We pay our respects to all Aboriginal and Torres Strait
Islander Elders, past and present.

Don's Party was first performed by the Australian Performing Group at the Pram Factory, Melbourne on 11 August 1971 with the following cast:

DON	Wilfred Last
KATH	Evelyn Krape
SIMON	Tony Taylor
JODY	Yvonne Marini
MAL	Bruce Knappett
JENNY	Lindy Davies
MACK	John Smythe
EVAN	Graham Hartley
KERRY	Ros Horin
COOLEY	Rod Moore
SUSAN	Kerry Dwyer

Director, Graeme Blundell
Designer, Craig Haire

A revised version of the play was presented at the Jane Street Theatre, Sydney, opening on 29 June 1972 with the following cast:

DON	Martin Harris
KATH	Pat Bishop
SIMON	Mervyn Drake
JODY	Wendy Blacklock
MAL	Allan Lander
JENNY	Judith Fisher
MACK	James H. Bowles
EVAN	Ken Shorter
KERRY	Darlene Johnson
COOLEY	John Ewart
SUSAN	Barbara Stephens

Set design by Lindsay Megarrity
Directed by John Clark

CHARACTERS

DON
KATH
SIMON
JODY
MAL
JENNY
MACK
EVAN
KERRY
COOLEY
SUSAN

All characters are in their early to middle thirties, with the exception of SUSAN, who is in her early twenties.

SETTING

The action of the play takes place in the home of DON and KATH HENDERSON in the Melbourne suburb of Lower Plenty. The set is constructed in such a way that the living room and the kitchen of the house can be viewed simultaneously. The living room is spacious, with trendy decor. The walls are hung with abstract prints and large, ceiling-high bookshelves are stacked with books.

The date is 25 October 1969: election night.

ACT ONE

8.40 p.m. Guests are expected any minute. DON *is in the kitchen. He plugs in the television set and begins to adjust it. The audience can't see the screen but can hear the soundtrack.* KATH *is tidying the living room.*

KATH: [*edgy, preoccupied*] Put the peanuts and crisps around, will you?

DON: I'm tuning in the television.

KATH: People will be arriving any minute.

DON: I'm tuning in the television.

KATH: Just switch it on and leave it.

DON: I'm adjusting the vertical hold.

KATH: [*barely controlled*] Just switch it on and leave it.

DON: The picture's rolling.

KATH: Well, it wasn't last night.

DON: Well, it is now.

KATH: Adjust the vertical hold.

DON: That's what I'm doing.

KATH: Could you come back to it? The guests'll be arriving any minute now.

DON: So what!

KATH: They might like something to eat!

DON: I'm adjusting the contrast.

[DON *turns up the sound on the* TV. *We hear this announcement:*]

TV: Polling closed tonight at eight o'clock and the counting of votes for the 1969 Federal Election has begun. We are now in the Central Tally Room in Canberra and as soon as the results come to hand we will bring them to you. Our panel of experts is standing by ready to interpret voting trends for you, and will be conducting interviews with party representatives throughout the evening. Stay tuned to this channel for a complete coverage of the 1969 Federal Election.

[KATH *glares at him, puts down whatever she's doing, picks up the trays of chips and Twisties, and starts distributing them herself in the living room, banging the trays down unnecessarily hard to give vent to her annoyance.* DON *stands back from the television set, satisfied that it's working.*]

DON: There's no need for you to do it.

KATH: I've done it.

DON: I would've done it.

KATH: [*sharply*] Try and act like a host tonight, will you?

DON: [*complaining*] Cut it out.

[DON *turns down the sound.*]

KATH: It wouldn't take much effort.

DON: Since when have I been rude to guests?

KATH: You usually point them in the direction of the fridge and that's it.

DON: That's all my friends need.

KATH: I can't see the point of coming to a party with the sole intention of drinking yourself into a stupor.

DON: That's not the intention.

KATH: Hmm.

DON: There's a bloody important event on the television tonight. Or perhaps you haven't heard.

KATH: It's just an excuse for a booze-up.

DON: [*flaring*] A booze-up? That's why I've been out there all day handing out how-to-vote cards? Just an excuse for a booze-up?

KATH: I've never noticed Cooley showing much interest in politics.
[*Pause.*]

DON: [*indignant*] Cooley's left of centre!

KATH: The only thing Cooley's left are a trail of used up women and more empty beer bottles than anyone else in Australia.
[*Pause.*]
Who's he bringing tonight?

DON: [*surly*] I don't know.

KATH: Is he bringing that air hostess?

DON: No.

KATH: What happened to her? She was nice.

DON: I don't know.

KATH: Probably got too serious.

DON: Probably.

KATH: Who's he bringing then?

DON: I told you. I don't know. He just flew down from Sydney yesterday.

KATH: Could you tell him to leave his gymnastics until he gets back to the motel? He woke Richard last time.

DON: He didn't wake him. The air hostess did.

KATH: It's frightening for a young child.

DON: It was probably frightening for the air hostess. Would you like a drink?

KATH: I can't. I'm on tablets.

DON: They were supposed to make you happy. Bloody shithouse tablets.

KATH: [*sharply*] Lay off. And try and show me a little bit of affection tonight, will you?

DON: I show you a lot of affection. You just don't notice it.

KATH: Neither does anyone else.

    [*Pause.*]

If you want the honest truth, I think that your friends are the biggest bunch of pricks I've ever met.

DON: Yeah… well, it would be a pretty sparse party if we threw one for your friends. Unless we invited the pottery class.

KATH: Why did you marry me if I'm so bloody mundane?

DON: I didn't want my personality swamped.

    [DON *moves to the record player and puts on the Beatles' "When I'm Sixty-Four".*]

KATH: As well as filling up the odd beer glass, try and make sure everyone mixes.

DON: Everyone knows each other.

KATH: Jody and Simon don't know anyone.

DON: That was a brilliant move, that was.

KATH: What?

DON: Inviting Simon and Jody.

KATH: Wasn't I supposed to invite any of my friends?

DON: Inviting those two to an election night party with my friends is equivalent to inviting Cooley to a Women's Liberation meeting. [*singing*]

> Will you still need me,
> Will you still feed me…
>
> [*The front doorbell rings.* KATH *goes to move.*]
>
> When I'm sixty-four…
>
> [*He goes to the door and ushers in* SIMON *and* JODY.]

[*jovially*] Simon. Jody. Long time no see. Can I take your coat?

> [DON *takes* JODY's *coat.* SIMON *is immaculately dressed and good looking, but his hair is fluffed up and set so perfectly that the effect is a little bit too effete and prissy. He has a cultivated confidence and bonhomie that covers a certain unease. This becomes more evident as the play progresses.* JODY *is attractive and socially confident. She has a conservative upper middle class background, which sometimes emerges as a trace of arrogance. She is very fashionably dressed.*]

As a matter of fact we were just talking about you.

SIMON: Nothing bad, I hope?

DON: On the contrary. We were saying that you'd both add a touch of refinement to the gathering. There'll be some pretty grotty types here.

JODY: I hope I haven't overdressed.

DON: No. You'll be right. Come and I'll get you a drink.

SIMON: [*handing* DON *two bottles of beer in the normal brown paper bag*] Whack these in the Westinghouse.

DON: Take them in yourself mate. I've just had a domestic with the wife.

> [SIMON *holds up a finger, the gesture suggesting that he knows the situation perfectly. He goes into the kitchen and ad libs a quiet conversation with* KATH *as he puts the beer into the fridge. The focus remains on* DON *and* JODY.]

JODY: I have overdressed, haven't I?

DON: [*grinning*] For Christ sake, woman, no one's going to give a stuff how you're dressed.

JODY: I've got plenty of casual gear in the wardrobe but I just didn't think. What sort of people are coming?

DON: Mainly friends of mine.

JODY: Will they all be Labor?

DON: They'll all be left wing.

JODY: I should have worn my casual gear.

DON: [*good humoured*] For Christ sake. If you say another word about your gear I'll do something drastic.

JODY: It's important for a woman to feel she's dressed appropriately.

DON: Right!

[DON *walks offstage toward the area of the bedroom.* SIMON *walks back into the living room.*]

SIMON: Where's Don going?

JODY: I don't know.

SIMON: Did he get you a drink?

JODY: No.

SIMON: No. He didn't get mine either.

KATH: [*from the kitchen*] Did Don get you a drink?

SIMON: No. I don't think he did.

KATH: Don. Would you pour your guests a drink?

JODY: He's not here.

KATH: [*muttering*] Where is he?

JODY: He went off towards the bedrooms.

KATH: [*annoyed*] I'll go and get him.

SIMON: I'll pour the drinks. It's no bother.

KATH: [*resuming her food preparation*] Would you, Simon? Thanks very much.

[SIMON *walks back into the kitchen.*]

You know what Don's like.

SIMON: [*pouring drinks*] Sometimes I think it's better to be a casual host.

KATH: Better for the host but not for the guests.

SIMON: I'm always so careful to be a good host that I miss all the action.

KATH: I wish Don would take a few lessons from you.

SIMON: Were you at our last barbecue?

KATH: No. I don't think we were.

SIMON: [*thinking*] I think we asked you… didn't we?

KATH: I think you did. I think Don had something on.

SIMON: That's right. He did. Pity you couldn't come. Vermouth and dry, Jody?

JODY: Please.

SIMON: Will you have something to drink, Kath?

KATH: No thanks. Not just yet.

SIMON: [*fidgeting*] Er… Kath…

KATH: Are you having trouble finding something?

SIMON: The dry…

KATH: [*blackly*] I told him to get dry.

SIMON: Look it doesn't matter. [*Raising his voice.*] Would you prefer a gin and bitter lemon, Jody?

JODY: Isn't there any vermouth and dry?

KATH: [*calling out sharply*] Don!

DON: [*offstage*] What?

KATH: Did you get the dry ginger?

JODY: Look it doesn't matter. Gin will be fine.

DON: [*offstage*] There's dry ginger there!

KATH: Where?

DON: [*off*] In the fridge.

SIMON: [*finding the dry ginger bottle*] Ah yes, here it is. A little bit of vermouth and a lot of dry for Jody.

   [*He pours a vermouth and dry and gives it to* JODY.]
Cold enough?

JODY: It's fine. How are you, Kath?

KATH: Fine. How are Sophie and Dalton?

JODY: Fine. How's Richard?

KATH: Fine. I'm sorry about this. I'll socialise a bit more when I get these done.

JODY: Home-made pizzas?

KATH: Mmm. Nothing very special.

JODY: They look delicious.

SIMON: We must try some of those for our next barbecue.

JODY: You'd have to bake them, wouldn't you?

SIMON: You could bake them inside.

JODY: What's the point of having a barbecue if you're going to bake things inside?

SIMON: Just because it's called a barbecue doesn't mean you have to barbecue everything.

KATH: [*looking round*] What's Don doing?

JODY: I don't know. He went inside.

[DON *walks into the living room. He has changed into a dinner suit, complete with dress shirt and black tie. He still wears brown casual shoes.*]

KATH: What's that in aid of?

DON: I've decided to embarrass everybody.

KATH: Take it off.

DON: No.

KATH: Take it off.

DON: I say, Simon old chap, where's your pornographic object?

SIMON: Where's my what?

DON: Where's your filthy object? Everyone had to make one—it was on the invitation.

SIMON: It's in the car. I'll get it.

[SIMON *goes out.*]

KATH: You can't stay dressed like that. Take it off for God's sake.

DON: Jesus, you're a humourless bitch.

[*He puts on an inappropriate record: 'Mr Wonderful' by Mantovani.*]

JODY: [*smoothing over*] He just did it to keep me company. I'm afraid I overdressed.

KATH: [*suddenly noticing*] What a gorgeous dress.

JODY: I was going to wear something casual.

KATH: I should have warned you; but for God's sake don't worry.

JODY: Do you think I ought to go home and change?

KATH: No I don't. Don's friends are nothing to worry about, I can assure you.

> [JODY *looks thoughtful.* SIMON *returns carrying a glued balsa structure that is vaguely phallic.*]

DON: Migod! What's that?

SIMON: I couldn't think of a name.

DON: It's supposed to be mind polluting. [*Looking at it.*] It might get a wood borer horny but it doesn't do much for me.

SIMON: It's an ambiguous stimulus. You read your lust into it.

DON: [*doing so*] I must be a bit short on lust.

> [*The doorbell rings.*]

Excuse me a second, Simon.

> [DON *goes to the door. The new arrivals are* MAL *and* JENNY. MAL *is tall, good looking, urbane and is dressed casually but thoughtfully.* JENNY *is attractive but has a biting quality of resentment about her, which often underlies her dialogue.* MAL *sees* DON's *dinner suit.*]

Come in.

MAL: [*commenting on the dinner suit and turning as if to go*] We must have the wrong address. What's the idea?

DON: I'm keeping my options open.

JENNY: If you're going to look like a gentleman, act like one.

> [DON *looks at her, not comprehending.*]

Take my wrap.

> [DON *bangs himself on the forehead as if to say, 'I knew there was something I should have offered to do', and helps her off with her wrap.*]

DON: [*to* MAL] How're things?

MAL: They'll be better after tonight.

DON: D'you think Gorton's going to go?

MAL: The Liberals are going to get it in the arse. I had a few beers with Whitlam's press secretary last Friday and he reckons Morgan's took another poll last weekend that gave Labor fifty-two percent. They were told to keep it quiet.

DON: Morgan's?

MAL: They do most of their work for the big dailies.

DON: That's incredible.

MAL: Hello, Kath.

[DON *has been tagging behind* MAL, *carrying* JENNY*'s coat, as they both step into the living room.*]

DON: Mal. Jenny. I'd like you to meet Simon and Jody.

[*They exchange perfunctory greetings.*]

MAL: [*talking to* DON *and ignoring the others*] Did you read that Gorton said that his low personal popularity was due to a well-organised smear campaign against him?

DON: [*grinning*] You wouldn't need to be much of an organiser. [*Laughing.*] I'll get you both a drink. Beer, Jenny?

[*He hands* KATH *the coat.*]

JENNY: Please.

DON: I wonder if you'd mind...

[KATH *exits with coat.* DON *goes, leaving* MAL *and* JENNY *and* SIMON *together. There is an awkward pause.*]

JENNY: That's a lovely dress... Jody, wasn't it?

JODY: That's right.

JENNY: I'm terrible with names.

JODY: I should've worn something more casual.

JENNY: [*shrugging*] Why? Looks fine.

SIMON: [*after a pause, to* MAL] I take it you'll be barracking for Labor tonight?

MAL: [*looking at him*] Well I don't anticipate yelling myself hoarse, but I'm certainly hoping for a change of government. I take it we all are?

SIMON: [*looking embarrassed*] Well... er... I'm... er... fairly neutral.

[KATH *returns.*]

KATH: [*breaking the silence*] How are the children, Jenny? [*To* SIMON *and* JODY.] Jenny's got four.

17

JENNY: The kids are fine. It's their father who's the pain in the arse.

JODY: [to KATH] I've been told that he's an intellectual. Do you think I could touch him?

JENNY: You can do what you like with him.

[JODY *touches* MAL *on the arm.*]

MAL: I'm touched.

[DON *returns with the drinks.*]

DON: Here we are.

[MAL *and* JENNY *thank him.*]
   Simon? Jody?

[JODY *shakes her head.*]

SIMON: Not just at the moment, thanks.

DON: [to MAL *and* JENNY] Jody actually admits to voting Liberal but Simon here claims that he is strictly neutral.

SIMON: [*smiling*] I'm a swinging voter.

MAL: Which way did you swing today?

SIMON: That, as they say, is between me and the ballot box.

MAL: [to JODY] And what about you, Jody? Are you a genuine Liberal?

JODY: That's right.

MAL: It's one thing to vote Liberal but another thing to admit it. I think you've very courageous.

JODY: That finishes me, doesn't it?

MAL: [*looking her up and down*] Not at all. It makes you very interesting.

[*He taps a large roll of paper he's carrying under his arm.*]
   Does anybody mind if I unroll my pornographic object?

JENNY: You'd all better laugh. He spent all afternoon on it.

MAL: [*as he unrolls it*] Charming wife I have.

[*The poster is a huge hand drawn copy of a Playboy cartoon showing an actor and an actress sitting naked on a bed in front of a large audience. The prompt is making frantic gestures. He is holding the thumb and forefinger of his left hand in a circle and reciprocating the forefinger of his right hand through this circle. Everyone laughs when they see it.*]

JENNY: He copied it from *Playboy.*

MAL: I *was* going to *tell* them that. [*Catching sight of* SIMON's *contribution.*] What's that?

SIMON: It's er... my contribution.

MAL: What is it?

DON: It's Simon's ambiguous stimulus. It gets very provocative when you've had a few beers.

MAL: [*looking at* DON *with a trace of a smirk*] Really? Hmmm.
[*The doorbell rings.*]
Have you got the television going?
[MAL *pins up his poster on the back wall. The doorbell rings. The new arrival is* MACK, *a dishevelled little man carrying a large poster and numerous bottles.*]
G'day, shithead. Where's that bitch of a wife of yours?

MACK: I've left her.

MAL: [*embarrassed*] Oh, I'm sorry... what... er... why...?

MACK: Why did I leave her? G'day Don, Kath. [*Seeing* JODY.] Who's this gorgeous woman?

DON: Oh... er, Simon and Jody I'd like you to meet Mack. He's just left his wife.

SIMON: [*extending his hand*] I'm sorry to hear that.

MACK: [*shaking his hand*] Shit, I'm not.
[*He unrolls his poster. It is a large photograph of a nude woman in a provocative pose.* KATH *glares at* DON.]

SIMON: Who's that?

MACK: My wife.
[SIMON *looks at* JODY.]
You wouldn't think she's a librarian, would you?

DON: [*explaining to* SIMON *and* JODY] Mack's a camera fanatic.
[MAL *and* MACK *pin up the photograph.*]

KATH: I'm not sure Ruth would like herself pinned up on our wall.

MACK: I don't care what she'd like.

MAL: You've really left her?

MACK: I've left her.

DON: When?

MACK: Three days ago.

KATH: Where are you living?

MACK: [*embarrassed*] I'm still at home.

> [*Pause.*]

> It was easier for her to shift out than me. [*Rubbing his hands together as if to signal 'Don't feel sorry for me'.*] Any results through?

DON: [*has had a quick look when he was out there pouring drinks*] Early signs of a swing but it'll be a while yet before you can really start to make predictions.

MACK: Have you been listening to Gair?

MAL: Academics brainwashing the students into radicalism?

DON: Did he say that?

MAL: Bloody oath he said it. He says a lot more in private too.

MACK: What?

MAL: Well, among other things that we shouldn't teach courses in sociology or politics because this is where the bulk of the activists come from.

MACK: Who was telling you that?

MAL: A reporter mate of mine who's covering the elections.

DON: That's incredible.

JODY: You must admit it's getting a bit much.

MAL: What is?

JODY: When I went to the University I went there to learn not to take over the place.

MACK: Look, I don't mean to be offensive, but you sound like a Young Liberal.

DON: Jody's a self-confessed right winger.

MACK: Come on. I've never met a person who voted Liberal in my life. Can't think why they keep winning.

JODY: Oh for heaven's sake. [*To* DON.] Is there some more vermouth in the kitchen?

DON: [*following her*] Look I'll... er... get it.

JODY: [*good naturedly*] I may as well learn where it is. You're not the most reliable of hosts.

MAL: Went there to learn? Is she serious?

MACK: [*nodding*] She needs a long hard... talking to.

[*They look at each other, nod and go off after her.* DON *pours* JODY*'s drink and the four of them engage in sporadic conversation.* MACK *and* MAL *try to get a response from* JODY *but she prefers to look at the election results being posted on the tally board. The focus, however, remains with* SIMON, JENNY *and* KATH *and during their interaction* JODY *is gradually drawn into conversation with the three males in the kitchen.*]

JENNY: [*breaking the awkward pause*] What do you do, Simon?

SIMON: Well, er...

KATH: Simon's an accountant.

JENNY: Oh yes.

SIMON: An industrial accountant.

JENNY: Oh yes. Is it interesting work?

SIMON: It can be quite absorbing. There's a lot of the humdrum in it, of course, but that's true of any job.

JENNY: What's your firm make?

SIMON: Plastic extrusions and polystyrene slabs.

[*Pause.*]

What's your husband do?

JENNY: He's a professional bullshit artist. [*As* SIMON *opens his mouth then shuts it again.*] A management consultant. [*Wincing and holding her forehead.*] I think I'm getting a migraine.

KATH: Could I get you some aspirins?

JENNY: No thanks, dear. The only thing for these is to sit down and keep still. Will you excuse me?

[*She goes and sits down.*]

SIMON: That's rotten luck. Does she often get migraines?

KATH: Only at our parties.

SIMON: [*trying to ignore the implications*] It could be the noise.

[MACK *sticks his head into the living room.*]

MACK: Simon, old cock. Do you mind if we tell your wife a dirty story?

SIMON: [*affably*] She's used to it.

MACK: [*to* JODY] He says you're used to it.

JODY: [*in mock indignation*] The bloody liar.

MACK: [*to* JODY] Have you heard the duck hunter?

JODY: [*innocent*] No.

DON: Come on. Give us the duck hunter, Mack.

MACK: No. [*Coy.*] It's too rude.

JODY: Go on.

MACK: No.

JODY: What's it about?

MACK: It's a story about a duck hunter.

JODY: I gathered that.

MACK: With actions.

MAL: I don't want to see anything disgusting.

MACK: [*remembering*] I've got to have a broom.
    [*He looks around.*]

JODY: [*giggling*] A broom? [As MAL *goes off to get a broom.*] Is it one
    of those jokes with actions?

MACK: Sort of. Have you ever been duck hunting?

JODY: No.

    [MAL *hands* MACK *the broom.*]

MACK: That's my rifle.

MAL: Duck hunters use shotguns.

MACK: I like to give the ducks a chance.

    [MAL *hands* MACK *a roll of toilet paper.*]

JODY: What's that?

MACK: That's my roll of toilet paper. All right. [*Pocketing the toilet
    paper.*] You've never been duck hunting?

JODY: No.

MACK: Well, you often have to wade through shallow lakes, so here's
    the duck hunter in big rubber boots, wading through the shallows,
    rifle at the ready, itching for a duck.
    [*He fills out his story with appropriate actions.*]
    Suddenly! Suddenly! He gets a feeling that he'd like to unburden

himself, so he puts the shotgun under his arm, undoes his belt, [*Doing so.*] and eases off his trousers. [*Doing so, then hesitating.*] No, it's too rude.

MAL: [*ushering them out of the kitchen*] We'll move to the privacy of the bedroom.

JODY: Migod. It must be foul.

> [*She goes along, nonetheless.* MACK *leads them, trousers still at half mast.*]

MACK: We'll just duck off to the bedroom. Single file.

> [*The others follow him in single file.*]

Wading, wading, wading, wading.

> [*They all make wading actions.* SIMON, JENNY *and* KATH *look at this procession with some disquiet. The three men usher* JODY *towards the bedroom, still wading. Just as they are reaching the top of the stairs* JENNY *yells.*]

JENNY: Mal!

> [*The duck hunters pause.*]

MAL: [*irritated*] What?

JENNY: Have you got a match?

MAL: [*patting his coat pocket perfunctorily*] No.

SIMON: [*getting the courage to throw in his bit*] Jody.

JODY: [*irritated*] What?

SIMON: I wonder if you could give the babysitter a ring to check whether the children are all right.

JODY: Ring her yourself.

SIMON: You know her better than I do.

> [*The embarrassing moment is broken when the front doorbell rings.* DON *goes to answer it.*]

DON: The phone's in the hall.

MACK: [*as a disgruntled* JODY *rings the babysitter*] I'll tell you the rest later.

DON: Kerry, darling…

> [*The new arrivals are* EVAN *and* KERRY. EVAN *is well groomed and subdued, almost brooding.* KERRY *is very attractive and*

has a touch of affectation in her voice. She tends to overreact emotionally. A touch of hysteria.]

KERRY: [*noting* DON'*s dinner suit*] Migod!

DON: I'm trying to embarrass my guests. G'day Evan. Good to see you both.

KERRY: Good to see you.

EVAN: How's the election going?

[*He hands* DON *a bottle of scotch.*]

DON: Looks like there's quite a swing. We're all keeping our fingers crossed. [*To* KERRY.] Can I take your coat?

[*They move towards the other guests.*]

KERRY: What *is* the idea of the dinner suit?

DON: [*shrugging*] Just a gimmick.

KERRY: Hello, Kath.

KATH: Hello Kerry, Evan.

DON: I don't think you know the other people here, do you?

[KERRY *and* EVAN *shake their heads.*]

Kerry and Evan… Simon, Mack, and Jenny over there in the chair. Simon's wife Jody is ringing up their babysitter and Jenny's husband Mal is out in the kitchen watching the election telecast. Come and meet Mal while I pour you a drink.

[DON, KERRY, EVAN *and* MACK *move to the kitchen.* SIMON, *for want of something to do, looks through the record collection.*]

Mal… Kerry and Evan.

MAL: Hullo, Evan…

[*He turns from the television to look, and is obviously knocked out by* KERRY.]

Kerry, was it?

[*He indicates the television: the sound isn't turned up, he is just watching the tally board.*]

Looks good at this stage. [*To* DON.] They are the right political shade I hope?

DON: [*grinning*] No worries.

MAL: Well, after that other pair I'm a bit wary.

DON: They're Kath's friends.

KERRY: [*looking at the screen*] Malcolm Mackay's in trouble.

DON: Thank Christ for that.

MAL: Lilley's going to be a cliff-hanger.

DON: Who's the sitting member there?

MAL: Kevin Cairns. If Mackay and Cairns went, the Liberals would lose their extreme right wing in one hit.

[JODY *walks back from the phone and sits down at a distance from* SIMON, *with whom she is still furious.* MAL *turns up the* TV.]

TV: With less than ten percent of the votes counted so far it is not yet possible to form an accurate picture of the likely state of the parties.

[*The remainder of the announcement overlaps the subsequent dialogue.*]

Early votes have come to hand from the ACT, Victoria, New South Wales, Tasmania and some of the Queensland seats. Polling in South Australia closed only a half an hour ago and no results have come through yet from that state. As Western Australian time is two hours behind Eastern Standard Time results are not expected from Western Australia until about ten o'clock tonight.

KATH: I don't think you've been here since we moved in, have you?

KERRY: No. [*Realising it is expected of her.*] I'd love to look over the place.

KATH: I'll show you round. Would you like to see the house, Evan?

EVAN: [*watching the telecast*] I'll have a wander round later, thanks Kath.

[KERRY *and* KATH *go.*]

KATH: It's nowhere near as interesting as your place, but we're starting to get it into some sort of shape at last.

KERRY: Sometimes I think we would have been better going into a new house. The plumbing in old houses is terrible.

[*They disappear into the back part of the house.*]

MAL: Bloody women.

[*He turns down the* TV.]

MACK: Ruth was just the same. I could never care less. As long as I had a roof over my head and the rain didn't come in I couldn't care less.

MAL: Right.

MACK: I know a couple who spend all their time doing renovations to their house. Crazy.

EVAN: I like renovating.

MACK: Well if you like it, fair enough.

EVAN: I like it.

DON: [*trying to cover up the awkward silence*] You've, er, really done something with that place, Evan. It was a complete bloody wreck when you started.

EVAN: [*flatly*] Yes, it's coming on.

DON: Have you finished building Kerry's studio yet?

EVAN: Yes. Just last week.

MAL: What do you do when you're not renovating, Evan?

EVAN: I'm a dentist.

SIMON: Which is another form of renovating really.
[*His attempted joke falls very flat.*]

EVAN: What about you?

MAL: I'm a psychologist.

EVAN: Private practice?

MAL: Management consultant. Does Kerry renovate?

EVAN: When she's got time. She paints.

MACK: Dabbles a bit in the oils?

DON: Dabbles? She's had three major exhibitions.

EVAN: Four. The Leveson Gallery last month.

DON: [*embarrassed*] That's right. I must apologise to her. She got very good crits, didn't she?

EVAN: Not really.

DON: [*embarrassed*] Oh, I, er, heard somewhere it was very successful.

EVAN: She sold a lot of stuff. She's very fashionable at the moment.

MAL: Do you find it a bit hard to keep up with the jargon?

DON: [*covering*] Evan is doing fine arts at the Uni as a single subject to get a bit of background.

MAL: Do you find it's helpful?

EVAN: [*tense*] I gave it up.

MAL: I've heard it's a pretty tough course.

EVAN: [*tenser*] It crapped me. Look, I forgot to bring in our party contribution!

DON: Not to worry. It was only a gag to get the party moving.

EVAN: No, look… I'll go and get it.

[*He leaves.*]

MACK: Who brung him?

MAL: What a superb woman.

DON: And doesn't she know it.

MAL: He'd have his hands full keeping her in check, wouldn't he?

DON: He doesn't.

MAL: She plays a bit?

DON: [*with a trace of bitterness*] As long as you're in the top ten in some branch of the arts.

MACK: [*to* MAL] Stick a paintbrush in your arsehole and see how you go.

MAL: [*to* DON] Have you ever had a go at her?

DON: What do you reckon?

MAL: No luck?

DON: Depends what you mean.

MAL: Come on. Yes or no?

DON: Yes… And then no.

[*They jostle* DON *and jeer at his lack of success.* DON *takes a beer bottle and goes into the living room to act the host.* MAL *turns up the* TV.]

TV: The most significant trend to counting has been the marked swing to Labor.

[MAL *and* MACK *cheer.*]

Eight percent, the biggest since the present party system came into operation. If this trend continues to midnight Labor will form the new Government.

[*Another cheer.* KERRY *and* KATH *come back from the bedrooms.*]

KERRY: [*re-entering with* KATH] It's a very convenient layout.

KATH: It's so flimsy compared with an old place.

KERRY: You ought to try cooking in my kitchen.

KATH: Yes it is a bit small.

KERRY: Evan's knocking out the whole back part and remodelling it. It's his next project.

KATH: That'll make things easier.

DON: Drink, Kerry?

KERRY: I'll go and get it.

> [*She goes towards the kitchen.* MAL *turns down the* TV.]

MAL: Hullo, Kerry. I hear that you're very creative.

KERRY: Thank you. Are you interested in art?

MAL: [*lying*] Very much.

MACK: [*looking at* MAL *as if to say, 'you bloody liar'*] I do a lot of photography.

KERRY: I've seen your photography.

MACK: It was worth a try. [*Taking her aside.*] Is your husband the jealous type?

KERRY: He's more the brooding type. Why?

MACK: To be quite frank, certain men at this party are going to offer themselves to you tonight.

KERRY: Well, I'm afraid that certain men are going to be disappointed.

MACK: Which ones?

> [SIMON *puts on a record. He puts it on too loud; the needle jumps and slides along the disc. There is some consternation.* SIMON *is embarrassed.* EVAN *returns carrying a rather good abstract print. It does not appear to be very pornographic.*]

EVAN: I forgot to bring in our contribution.

KATH: Look, you shouldn't have done anything like this.

EVAN: It should go with your colour scheme.

DON: That's not pornographic.

EVAN: It wasn't meant to be.

MACK: What have you got against pornography?

EVAN: What have you got against art?

> [MACK *cannot find an answer.*]

KATH: We'll hang it in our bedroom. Come and have a look.

EVAN: [*to* DON] After you.

DON: [*who hadn't intended to go*] Right.

> [*They move off towards the bedroom.* KERRY, *who has left* MACK *to look at the exhibits, has now moved on into the kitchen.*]

KERRY: [*pointing to the* TV] How's it going?

MAL: [*academic, impressive*] Touch and go, but I'd have a dollar or two on a new government by midnight.

KERRY: Really? That's super.

MAL: I was speaking to Gough last week. He said if we get Evans, we've got the lot.

KERRY: What do you do?

MAL: Executive selection. I'm a psychologist.

KERRY: I've always been interested in psychology. Do you find that you're always analysing people?

MAL: [*enjoying playing the big psychologist*] All the time. It's an occupational hazard.

KERRY: What can you tell about me?

MAL: As a psychologist, I can't help feeling that your physical beauty would bring its problems.

KERRY: In what way?

MAL: Well, speaking fairly brutally, your attractiveness constitutes a sought-after commodity.

KERRY: So?

MAL: So you'd have no shortage of alternative offers which could place your marriage under some strain.

KERRY: I know a lot of attractive women who have stable marriages.

MAL: Of course, of course. It depends on the woman.

KERRY: In what way?

MAL: Well, to some women it's a very real cost to deny themselves the excitement of a new affair.

KERRY: I suppose you're right.

MAL: It's very clear to me that you're the type of woman who would resent being unable to act on her emotions.

KERRY: How do you deduce that?

MAL: It's a feeling I've got.

KERRY: A feeling?

MAL: I feel certain, for instance, that if I said to you that I'm very attracted to you and I'd be delighted if we had an affair, that you wouldn't reject it out of hand, but that depending on how you felt about me, you'd consider it.

KERRY: I would.

[Pause.]

MAL: You know of course that I would like to have an affair with you, so I'll be frank and say just that.

KERRY: That you'd like to have an affair with me?

MAL: Yes. How does that appeal to you?

KERRY: I'm afraid it doesn't.

MAL: Well that's... er... very frank of you.

KERRY: That reminds me. I must go and ask Evan whether he made up those frames today. Could you excuse me a second.

[She goes.]

MACK: [cheerfully] Can't win 'em all.

MAL: The night isn't over yet, boy.

[They watch the box in silence. The doorbell rings. DON emerges from the back of the house to answer it, followed by KATH and EVAN.]

DON: Here comes the floorshow.

[The new arrivals are COOLEY and SUSAN. COOLEY is very well dressed, but has the air of a larrikin about him. SUSAN is warmly attractive and much younger than COOLEY. COOLEY is carrying what appears to be an enormous carton of grog.]

COOLEY: [to DON] G'day, cunt features.

DON: [looking a little alarmed, glancing at SUSAN for her reaction] That's a nice way to greet an old friend.

COOLEY: A cunt is an object of joy. This is Susan.

[He points at DON's dinner suit and laughs raucously.]
Who are you trying to fool?

30

[COOLEY *has already barged on past* DON *to deposit the large carton on the floor. He withdraws two bottles of beer from it. He chuckles at his joke and hands the beer to* DON. DON *nods at* SUSAN, *she at him.*]

[*surveying the gathering*] Weak looking bunch of poofters. Where's Mack?

DON: In the kitchen.

COOLEY: Is Ruth with him?

DON: He's left her.

COOLEY: Yeah? [*Seeing* KERRY.] Hey. She's all right. Might have a go at that later.

[DON *looks anxiously at* SUSAN, *who must have heard this, but she smiles benignly.*]

DON: Er, did you bring a pornographic object?

COOLEY: [*patting* SUSAN] Here she is. Where's Mal?

DON: In the kitchen.

COOLEY: [*seeing* JENNY] G'day Jenny, you old fishwife. Cracked it for another migraine?

JENNY: I hope you get one one day.

COOLEY: [*looking at* SIMON] Who's the poofter with the poker up his arse?

DON: Simon Bascombe. That's his wife Jody.

COOLEY: [*appraising her*] Slight stir of the brooding monster.

[MACK *has heard* COOLEY'*s entry. He enters the living room.* MAL *follows a short while later when the greeting ritual is under way.*]

MACK: [*disguising affection with coarseness*] It had to be Cooley.

COOLEY: My God. It's Mickey Mouse. How are you, you little prick?

MACK: None the better for seeing you, you great turd.

DON: [*to* SUSAN] Charming language when these two get together.

[SUSAN *merely smiles warmly.*]

COOLEY: Shitting, shagging and shaving. Same old routine.

MACK: Life gets a bit monotonous, doesn't it?

[MAL *appears.*]

MAL: Don't tell me.

COOLEY: There's a bullshit artist at every party and this one's no exception.

MAL: There goes that flashing wit again.

DON: Come and I'll introduce you.

COOLEY: I'll introduce myself. Just get me a beer. What about some music? Susan wants to get her gear off. What do you want, darling?

SUSAN: 'Satisfaction'!

COOLEY: You should complain? [*Striding over to the record player and putting the record on.*] This is more like a morgue than a party. Let's hear it.

[SUSAN *looks up at* DON *and begins to take off her coat. He realises she wants him to help her out of it and jerks apologetically into action.* COOLEY *is doing a solo by himself and singing the words to boot.* SUSAN *smiles at* DON, *who out of politeness asks* KATH *to dance.* MAL *out of lechery goes up to* KERRY, *but* EVAN *has beaten him to it. He goes and dances with* JODY. SIMON, *out of politeness, goes and asks* JENNY, *but she pleads headache. He stands there uncertainly, puffing his pipe during the number.*]

Don! Where's my beer!

DON: [*in the kitchen*] I'm looking at the telecast.

COOLEY: [*feigning innocence*] Is something on the television?

KERRY: How's it going?

DON: It's still looking very good, very good. Come and have a look. Hey, it's very close—it's in the balance. Come and have a look, everybody. It's touch and go.

[*The others move to the kitchen to watch, with the exception of* JODY.]

Turn it down, Mal.

[MAL *turns down the record.*]

TV: The outcome of the 1969 Federal Election hangs in the balance. At the present stage of counting the Liberal/Country Party Coalition is certain of winning fifty-three seats and the ALP fifty-four with eighteen of the one hundred and twenty-five seats in doubt.

[*While the others listen to the* TV *announcement,* MAL *puts on a softer, more lyrical record. He returns to* JODY *and asks her to continue dancing. The sound from the* TV *set and the light in the kitchen fade.*]

MAL: You really do vote Liberal?

JODY: Mmm.

MAL: [*dancing close to her*] Why?

JODY: It's a purely emotional thing. I associate Labor with coarse men in overalls.

MAL: Labor's not just a trade unionists' party anymore.

JODY: I know. It's just an emotional thing.

MAL: [*hand stealing down onto her bum*] You tend to follow our emotions.

JODY: Yes. Would you mind taking your hand off my bottom?

MAL: [*moving closer*]What'll you do if I don't?

JODY: Knee you in the balls.

MAL: I'm sure you wouldn't.

[*She does.* MACK *has just left the kitchen and sees it.* MAL, *angry and in pain, retreats to the patio.*]

MACK: [*laughing*] I saw it all, boy. You were feeling her arse. [*To* JODY.] Dance with me. I'm not nearly as offensive as him. [*Dancing close.*] Nice music to dance to.

[*He puts his hand on her bum.*]
Take it off.

MACK: [*not taking his hand off*] Very pleasant music, isn't it?

JODY: You saw what happened to him.

MACK: I think you should take things into account.

JODY: What things?

MACK: [*still with his hand on her bum*] Well my… [*Shrugging.*] wife.

JODY: What's that got to do with your hand on my bottom?

MACK: When you've had an emotional shock you need something tangible to hang on to.

[JODY *looks at him bemused, takes his hand and shifts it to halfway up her back. For the rest of their interaction, however, it slips back to its original position—after a reasonable time-lapse.* JODY *makes no objection.*]

MACK: [*becoming serious*] I suppose it had to come. There was something a bit unhealthy about our relationship.

JODY: What do you mean?

MACK: To be quite honest, I've got to accept a lot of the blame for the failure of our marriage.

JODY: You're being very fair.

MACK: I'm being more than fair. She's a bitch. Did you know I take photographs?

JODY: Yes. I've seen the picture of your wife.

MACK: Quite honestly, I've got to shoulder a lot of the blame for the failure of our relationship.

JODY: You just said that.

MACK: No, in all seriousness, I'm a little bit off.

JODY: How do you mean?

MACK: About sex.

JODY: We're all a little bit off if only we faced up to it.

MACK: Do you think so?

JODY: I think we'd all be surprised at the sort of things Mr and Mrs Average do in the privacy of the bedroom.

MACK: Do you and Simon…?

JODY: I'm sure *they* do.

MACK: I still think I'm a little bit off.

JODY: Nonsense.

MACK: I used to take a lot of suggestive photos of my wife.

JODY: She should have been flattered.

MACK: I used to hang them all round the walls of our house.

JODY: Sort of bra and panty photos?

MACK: Some.

JODY: What else?

MACK: You'll think I'm off.

JODY: No I won't.

MACK: I wanted her to seduce my friends.

JODY: [*a little taken aback*] Really!

MACK: That's unusual, isn't it?

JODY: [*doubtfully*] No…

MACK: And take photos from the cupboard… without their knowing.

JODY: Did she do it?

MACK: [*in his defence*] Yes… but she wouldn't let me take the photos.
[*Pause.*]

JODY: I'd be… flattered if Simon wanted… er … to take some photos of me.
[*Pause.*]

MACK: Has he got a camera?

JODY: No.

MACK: Well… he could borrow mine. I won't be… using it for a while.
[*During the last part of this dialogue* SIMON *has emerged from the kitchen and stands there puffing on his pipe. He notes the position of* MACK's *hand.* MACK *and* JODY *don't notice him until he moves closer and they almost bump into him.*]

SIMON: [*coughing*] Hello there.

MACK: [*embarrassed, moving his hand*] Hello. Did you want to dance with your wife?

SIMON: No. Go ahead.
[*Embarrassed silence.* MACK *and* JODY *begin to dance again. But he stays there.*]

JODY: [*annoyed by his presence*] Did you want something?

SIMON: Did the children go down all right?

JODY: [*tersely*]] Yes. [*To* MACK.] Would you excuse me for a moment?
[*She leaves.* SIMON *and* MACK *stand there awkwardly.*]

SIMON: What… er… do you do for a living?

MACK: I'm a design engineer.

SIMON: Really?

MACK: What about you?

SIMON: I'm one of those chaps who keeps a watchful eye on you.

MACK: Are you from ASIO? [*Seeing* SIMON's *look.*] Just joking.

SIMON: I'm an industrial accountant.

MACK: [*uninterested*] Oh yes.

SIMON: [*rising to the balls of his feet and trying to think of something to say*] Did you get along to the film festival this year?

MACK: No.

SIMON: [*embarrassed*] I, er, thought, with your interest in photography you might have gone.

MACK: I, er, only take still stuff. Different sort of thing.

SIMON: Yes. [*Looking at* MACK'*s photos of his wife.*] I suppose in a way you could say that a movie was nothing but a series of stills.

MACK: Yes, well… they both use a lens. It's just that the, er, movie keeps, er… [*Making hand motions.*] moving. Look. This bloody beer mug of mine—whenever it runs dry, it rears up and drags me to the kitchen.

> [MACK *moves to the kitchen. The* TV *fades up. The commentary is just audible during the following scenes.* KERRY *moves out of the kitchen.* MAL *returns from the patio and goes to her.*]

MAL: [*to* KERRY] We meet again.

KERRY: So I see.

COOLEY: [*joining them*] Why don't you introduce me, Malcolm?

MAL: [*glaring at* COOLEY] Kerry. This is, er, Grainger Cooley.

COOLEY: [*to* KERRY] You've heard of me, no doubt?

KERRY: [*smiling*] I'm afraid I haven't.

MAL: You should've heard of Kerry.

COOLEY: Why? What's she do?

MAL: She's an artist.

COOLEY: So's Susan.

KERRY: Does she paint?

COOLEY: No. She strips. She's really good.

MAL: A stripper?

COOLEY: Part time. She's an arts student at Sydney Uni. How about that! Brains and body.

MAL: [*to* KERRY] Grainger's got a very exotic taste in women.

COOLEY: She's working her way through college.

KERRY: It must be pretty exhausting for her.

COOLEY: It is. Specially since she met me.

[MAL *looks towards the ceiling as if to say 'My God'.*]

[*to* KERRY] What sort of things do you paint?

KERRY: I'm getting very interested in texture.

COOLEY: Texture, eh? Well, I'll see you again later. Got to have a word with the little man over there.

[COOLEY *moves across to speak to* MACK.]

They tell me you've left your wife?

MACK: She left me.

COOLEY: Yeah? Well you're better off without her. With all due respect, boy, and I've never said this up to now, but your wife is one of the great bourgeois monsters of our time.

MACK: Bourgeois? She let herself be photographed in the nude and hung up all around the house. That's bourgeois?

COOLEY: Now, come on. Don't get nostalgic about the bitch.

MACK: It s all right for you, mate.

COOLEY: Well, what do you want to do? Build her a shrine?

MACK: Well, bugger me, she was pretty tolerant.

COOLEY: Tolerant? She was tolerant all right. Under normal circumstances I'd never tell you this, but if you're going to go around eulogising her I might as well tell you that she screwed me, and I use the word advisedly. I was bloody near dragged to bed.

MACK: [*dully*] Yeah.

COOLEY: [*nodding his head in a self-satisfied way*] Digest that!

MACK: You digest this. I've got a whole roll of film of you performing, taken on my hundred and twenty millimetre Hasselblad, on triple-X Kodak, using available light.

COOLEY: [*taken aback*] Wha—Di—

MACK: They came up a bit grainy when I enlarged them, but you've got to expect that with a super-fast film.

COOLEY: [*angry*] You better be joking.

[JODY *returns.*]

MACK: [to JODY] Glad you called. This is a very old and a very bad friend of mine: Grainger Cooley, Jody… Grainger.

[COOLEY *smiles at her and nods, but he is still preoccupied with* MACK *'s confession about the photographs.*]

COOLEY: [*blackly*] Did you really take photographs?

MACK: Don't come on all pious, cock. You were screwing my wife.

COOLEY: For Christ's sake! You don't need to discuss it in public.

JODY: I'll come back later.

MACK: You stay right here.

COOLEY: A joke's a joke. But you don't set a friend up like that.

MACK: Shut up or I'll name you as co-respondent.

[*He moves off.* EVAN *has rejoined* KERRY. MAL *has moved off.* COOLEY *nods to* KERRY *and* EVAN, *intending to pass, but* KERRY *speaks to him.*]

KERRY: Oh, er, Grainger. Have you met my husband, Evan?

COOLEY: No. I haven't. How are you?

EVAN: Fine. I believe you're a lawyer.

COOLEY: Some of my clients don't. What about you?

EVAN: I'm a dentist.

COOLEY: [*nodding*] I've been hearing that your wife's very creative.

KERRY: I wish the critics thought so.

COOLEY: Why, have they been panning you?

KERRY: Faint praise.

EVAN: Moderate praise.

COOLEY: [*ogling* KERRY] If I was a critic you wouldn't be getting faint praise. What are they all? Poofters?

KERRY: [*smiling*] Not exactly.

COOLEY: Do they ever proposition you?

KERRY: The critics?

COOLEY: Yeah.

EVAN: It's not really as corrupt as all that.

COOLEY: If I was a critic and I came to review some hot young chick's etchings, it'd be a case of 'No root, no review'.

EVAN: You must conduct an interesting law practice.

COOLEY: [*shaking his head*] I'm taking a hammering tonight. I'll just go over and see Jenny. I can't lose that one. [*Going to* JENNY.] On my right, sour as a crab-apple jelly we have…

JENNY: [*grinning despite herself*] You took long enough to come and speak to me.

COOLEY: You're lucky I came to speak to you at all.

JENNY: Why's that?

COOLEY: I don't make a habit of speaking to hostile bitches in corners.

JENNY: Well, I don't make a habit of speaking to incorrigible lechers.

COOLEY: [*grinning*] Any man who isn't married with four kids is a lecher in your book, you flop-bellied, breast-sucked old lubra.

JENNY: Honestly, Grainger, your taste in women is becoming more adolescent as the years go by.

COOLEY: [*indignant*] Now just a minute. Susan is very intelligent.

JENNY: Come on. Big tits. Cow eyes. Vacuous chatter. I think you've started your middle-aged virility fantasies already. What happened to your air hostess? She was nice.

COOLEY: She had what they call a virgin cortex. No original thought had ever penetrated.

JENNY: [*laughing*] Grainger!

COOLEY: And then there was a beautiful socialite.

JENNY: What was wrong with her?

COOLEY: Her friends told her I was uncouth and boorish. Me? Two terms at Melbourne Grammar!

JENNY: The older you get, the younger your women get.

COOLEY: [*thinking*] When I was seventeen I stuffed a fifty year old barmaid in my old man's pub. It was pretty sordid but she just kept saying, 'Thank you, thank you', right through. How's your old man treating you?

JENNY: A lot of it's my fault. I'm a real bitch to him sometimes.

COOLEY: Mmm.

JENNY: Aren't I?

COOLEY. I'm neutral.

JENNY: He's following that Kerry woman around like a puppy dog.

COOLEY: I wouldn't worry.

JENNY: All I'm worried about is him making a fool of himself. Her husband's in a real shit.

COOLEY: There's nothing to worry about. It's the bastards that smile and shake your hand as you tickle their wives arses that you've got to watch.

JENNY: Well, you'd know.

COOLEY: [*patting her affectionately on the shoulder*] I'll just go and get myself a beer.

> [*He walks off. The* TV *has faded out. A record is playing.* DON, *who has been acting the host and filling up beer glasses, has also been gathering the courage to go and sit next to* SUSAN. *He does so just as* COOLEY *leaves* JENNY.]

DON: Have you, er, known Cooley long?

SUSAN: No, not long.

DON: He's a funny guy. He always puts on a turn at parties. I've known the bastard for fifteen years and every bloody party we're at, he... always puts on a turn...

SUSAN: [*looking at him*] Mmm.

> [*Pause.*]

I'm a full-time student and a part-time dancer. Is that what you were going to ask?

DON: I'm a teacher.

SUSAN: Are we going to sit round all night or are we going to be honest?

DON: [*embarrassed*] Let's, er, be honest.

SUSAN: Right.

DON: Are, er, you going to be in town long.

SUSAN: [*shaking her head*] I'm flying back tomorrow.

DON: You're only here for the night, then?

> [SUSAN *nods her head with a half smile on her face.*]

[*seeing her smile*] I'm not very good at this sort of thing

SUSAN: What are the ground rules around here?

DON: What do you mean?

SUSAN: What would happen if we were open about it?

DON: Who to?

SUSAN: Your wife.

DON: [*looking worried*] Jesus.

SUSAN: What if I said to her that there was some chemistry there. It's purely physical. I'm flying back to Sydney in the morning. No worries.

DON: [*worried*] I think she's a bit insecure.

> [MAL, *still trying to get his hands on something, comes up to them.* DON, *a little relieved to have someone else in the conversation, introduces him.*]

Susan. This is Mal.

> [SUSAN *nods her head.*]

MAL: You came with Cooley?

SUSAN: That's right. And you?

MAL: My wife. She's the bitch in the hostile stupor over there in the corner.

DON: She doesn't look quite herself tonight.

MAL: [*to* DON] One thing that really shits me about you, boy, is your compulsive politeness. My wife looks exactly herself tonight.

SUSAN: [*to* DON] She looks as if she could bite the balls off Mohammed Ali. I just love her. She's really fierce.

MAL: You ought to be married to her.

SUSAN: Why is she like that?

MAL: Don't ask me.

SUSAN: She's probably frustrated.

DON: That's what the problem is, Mal!

MAL: I didn't come here to have aspersions cast on my masculinity. I came here to admire Susan at close range.

DON: [*embarrassed, getting up to leave*] Well I'll... er...

SUSAN: [*putting a gentle but restraining hand on* DON's *knee*] Stay here.

MAL: We don't need him.

SUSAN: I need him.

MAL: What's he got that I haven't?

SUSAN: The nod.

MAL: You're joking.

SUSAN: I think he's beautiful. Don't you?

MAL: No.

SUSAN: Fair enough. Let's face it. If one person turned everybody on and another person turned nobody on then things would get a bit grim emotionally. Wouldn't they?

MAL: Kath will kill him.

[*He goes to the kitchen.*]

SUSAN: I don't see why she should. If the whole thing's made clear and open then I don't see why she should. [*To* DON.] Which one's your wife?

[DON *points her out.*]

Let's try it.

DON: I think she's a bit insecure.

SUSAN: Have you ever tried simple honesty with her?

DON: No, I, er…

SUSAN: I bet you've crept away and done it on the sly, though.

DON: Well, I've, er, yes, I've had affairs.

SUSAN: Have you felt good about it?

DON: No.

SUSAN: Well, let's try.

[*She gets up and goes across to* KATH. DON *follows her nervously and reluctantly.*]

Kath. My name's Susan.

[SUSAN *looks at* DON, *who looks away, and back at* SUSAN *and nods.* MAL *savours the situation in the background.*]

I was just admiring your décor.

KATH: It's a bit *House-and-Garden*ish.

SUSAN: Not really.

KATH: The trouble with décor is that if your tastes change after you've done it then you're stuck with it.

[DON, *unable to face the situation, moves off to a distance and shuffles through the records.*]

SUSAN: I'd probably go for something a bit simpler myself, but in this sort of thing it's all a matter of taste.

[*Pause.*]

I've, er, been talking to Don.

KATH: Yes. I saw.

SUSAN: He's a nice guy.

KATH: Sometimes.

SUSAN: I think you're really lucky

KATH: We have our bad times.

SUSAN: Are you, er, very jealous of him?

KATH: No.

SUSAN: I'm, er, flying back with Cooley tomorrow. Don and I, er…

KATH: Yes?

SUSAN: Look, it's purely physical. I'll, er, be gone tomorrow.

> [*Long pause.*]

KATH: Don?

> [SUSAN *nods.*]

You'd better ask *him*, hadn't you?

SUSAN: I thought I'd like to find out how you felt.

KATH: [*a trifle tersely*] It's nothing to do with me. He'll have to make up his own mind.

> [*She moves away.* SUSAN *goes across to* DON.]

DON: What'd she say?

SUSAN: She said it was your decision.

DON: How did she take it?

SUSAN: I don't think she was wrapped

DON: She's on anti-depressants.

SUSAN: Why didn't you tell me?

DON: I suppose I should've.

SUSAN: You'd better go and talk to her.

DON: Yes I, er, will.

> [DON *goes to approach* KATH *but she gives him a most pro-nounced cold shoulder. He hasn't the courage to persevere and goes to the television set where* EVAN *and* SIMON *have gravitated.*]

How's it going now?

EVAN: I think everything hinges on Western Australia.

DON: When will the first results come through from there?

EVAN: Another half hour or so. If the ALP goes down it'll be Victoria that does it.

DON: How's the DLP vote running?

EVAN: In Victoria?

[DON *nods.*]

Over ten percent.

[DON *shakes his head in disgust and wanders out with a bottle of beer in his hand.*]

SIMON: Do, er, you know many people here, Evan?

EVAN: Only Don and Kath.

SIMON: Yes, er, so do we. Are the others mainly, er, Don's friends?

EVAN: Apparently.

SIMON: They're, er, very, er, extroverted types, aren't they?

EVAN: I can't stand them.

SIMON: [*brightening visibly*] Well, I'm glad somebody else feels that way. Are you very interested in this election?

EVAN: Not much.

[SIMON *turns down the* TV.]

SIMON: [*even brighter*]I can't get up much enthusiasm about it either.

EVAN: If Labor gets in we might get a slightly better health scheme, slightly better social services and that's about it.

SIMON: And you're never sure how they're going to pay for it.

EVAN: They could take some more money from us for a start.

SIMON: What, more tax?

EVAN: I don't know what you're earning, but I pull in over twenty thousand dollars a year clear. On that sort of salary I can send my kids, [*Ruefully.*] if ever I have any, to the best schools, I can take out oodles of insurance, and because it's all tax deductible it costs me about half the price of someone on a low wage. That's not bad for extracting the odd molar, is it?

SIMON: Are you a socialist?

EVAN: Yes. Aren't you?

SIMON: [*not wishing to lose his newly found friend*] Well, I think all of us are socialists at heart.

[*Pause.*]

Unfortunately, it seems that the old profit motive seems to keep the economy moving.

EVAN: I think we better stop discussing politics or I'll end up landing you one on the jaw. [*Offering a bottle.*] Would you like a beer?

SIMON: [*accepting it*] Thanks.

[*They watch the television in silence. Even though it is only of mild interest to them they find it preferable to facing the party again.* MAL, *returning from the toilet, makes his way towards* JODY *and* MACK. *He is in the mood for a fight.*]

MAL: [*to* JODY] I'm afraid your party's in trouble.

JODY: I suppose a change of government wouldn't do any great harm.

MAL: It might even do some good. [*Tossing his hand.*] Oh, only in small things like health, education…

MACK: Shut up, shithead.

MAL: [*showing the effects of alcohol*] What? I can't have a serious political discussion. Is that a rule of the house, is it? I'm sorry. I forgot. A party is for frivolity and fun. Did you hear the one about the Grenadier Guardsman and the tourist lady?

MACK: [*to* JODY] How old is your youngest?

MAL: [*to* JODY] The thing that gets me about you people is the way you never think about what you're doing in life.

JODY: We've got a very clear idea of what we're doing.

MAL: You've got clear ideas [*Tapping his skull.*] planted straight into your skulls by some advertising copywriter.

JODY: Rot.

MAL: Would it be true to say that you are just about to sell your thirty thousand dollar house and take out a mortgage for a fifty thousand dollar house?

JODY: We've been thinking about it. How did you know that?

MAL: [*waving his finger tipsily*] Never mind. What are your motives for this particular piece of insanity?

MACK: [*to* JODY] Do you want me to hit him with my beer mug?

JODY: [*to* MAL] I'm thinking of having another baby.

MACK: [*to* JODY] You don't have to answer him.

JODY: I'll answer him.

MAL: Can't you get pregnant in a thirty thousand dollar house? Too cheap and nasty?

JODY: If we end up with three or four children we want plenty of space.

MAL: Haven't you got three or four bedrooms already?

JODY: It's not just the bedrooms. We'd like a music room and a play room and a study for Simon.

MAL: A music room and a play room and a study for Simon...!

JODY: If one child wants to play the piano and the other wants to play the radiogram we'd like them to be able to do it.

MAL: And if one of them wants to fly to the moon you'll have a space-ship there in the back yard. It's all bullshit. There is one reason and one reason alone why you are moving from a thirty thousand dollar home and that is status. S.T.A.T.U.S.

MACK: My God. He can spell.

MAL: [*to* MACK] Look you! If you want to contribute to this debate, contribute! If not, piss off!!

MACK: Debate? This isn't a debate, it's a bloody lecture! Sociology I!

JODY: It's got nothing to do with status!

MAL: Like hell it hasn't.

JODY: [*steamed up*] Are you usually as rude to people as you are at the moment?

[MACK *nods 'Yes' in the background, not to anyone in particular.*]

MAL: What do you expect when you come here trumpeting your conservatism as if God should kiss your arse for it?

JODY: I didn't trumpet it!

MAL: At least Simon had the grace to lie that he was neutral.

SIMON: [*indignant*] I wasn't lying!

[*The argument is attracting spectators.* DON *watches with interest, ignoring* KATH's *eye-signs to go and break it up.*]

MAL: I'm sorry. I take that back.

SIMON: I wasn't lying!

MAL: All right! All right!

SIMON: When somebody calls me a liar I believe I'm entitled to object.

MAL: That's right. Perfectly entitled. Now shut up. I'm arguing with your wife. [*To* JODY.] It would never occur to you to scale down your level of personal consumption. Earn less money and enjoy life more! [*Swinging around to* SIMON.] Peabrain!

JODY: [*to* DON] I'm sorry, Don, but when discussion degenerates to the level of personal abuse it's time to leave.

MAL: Personal abuse?

SIMON: What do you think calling me a peabrain is?

MAL: Accurate!

DON: [*to* MAL, *trying hard to keep back the trace of a grin*] Cut it out, shithead!

MAL: Well, he is a fucking peabrain.

SIMON: Cut that out!

MAL: What?

SIMON: If you have to resort to bad language to express yourself then you can't have much of a vocabulary!

MAL: Vocabulary? I've forgotten more words than you've ever learned! What's the meaning of evanesce?

SIMON: Really.

MAL: Pendulous, coruscate, ochlocracy, paplionaceous?

SIMON: I don't have to indulge in word games

MAL: What's the meaning of didactic?

SIMON: In the manner of a teacher.

MAL: Aha! Teased you out with an easy one.

SIMON: What's the meaning of obfuscate?

MAL: Come off it.

SIMON: Don't you know it?

MAL: Of course I do. I'd be very surprised if you did though.

SIMON: Of course I know. I asked it.

MAL: What's it mean, then?

SIMON: You're just trying to get out of it.

MAL: Get out of nothing. The whole point is that I wasn't arguing with you in the first place. [*Turning to* JODY.] All I wanted to know was why you made such a big issue of your conservatism.

JODY: Why are you making such an issue out of me making such an issue out my conservatism?

MAL: That's not relevant.

JODY: It's a new bloody question.

MAL: It's no sense arguing with you. You can't even follow the thread.

JODY: Pick on someone your own size!

COOLEY: Tell a quick joke, Mack.

MACK: Did you hear the one about Cinderella?

MAL: [*sourly*] At twelve o'clock her Tampax changed to a...

MACK: Have I ever told you about the time I met Cooley in the Walkabout Bar at the International?

MAL: No. Thank Christ.

MACK: I got this telegram on a Thursday. Arriving tomorrow TAA Flight 845. Seven-thirty. Meet at Cockpit. Cooley. Out of the blue. Too bad if I'd arranged to do anything else.

COOLEY: We'd arranged it all weeks before.

MACK: As it turns out I was pretty glad because Ruth was all set to cart me off for compulsory culture.

COOLEY: Philistine.

MACK: I've got nothing against the old Mozart but I'd rather have him emerge from the stereo while I'm into some steak and a bit of red, but you can imagine how Ruth reacted to the news. Made my day!

COOLEY: Made your day! When I saw you, you were still quivering with fear!

MACK: Crap! We went straight to the bar at the Walkabout and ordered a beer.

SIMON: I thought it was a restaurant.

MAL: [*still fuming*] There's a bar on one floor and a restaurant next to it.

SIMON: Aren't you confusing it with the cafeteria downstairs?

MAL: No, I'm not. [*Pronouncing each word deliberately.*] There is a bar in the Walkabout!

COOLEY: [*dogmatic, sending up* MAL] There is a bar in the Walkabout!

[*Politely, as* MAL *wheels around.*] It's right over in the far corner.

MACK: We'd hardly got the smell of hops into our nostrils when Cooley announces that he's randy.

COOLEY: [*mock incredulous*] Me? The very first words he said were: [*Doing a Peter Lorre imitation.*] 'Let's get ourselves a screw, Cools.' Not, 'How are you, how's your Aunt Dimitri?' 'Let's get ourselves a screw.'

MACK: That's crap.

COOLEY: My success with women affects this little prick. Every time he sees me it's like a conditioned reflex. [*Imitating again.*] 'Let's get ourselves a screw, Cools.'

MACK: The point is that, as we cast our eyes over to the restaurant half of the deal, we saw these two magnificent waitresses.

COOLEY: Absolute ratshit. The bottom of the barrel.

MACK: I seem to remember you being quite enthusiastic at the time.

COOLEY: You're my friend. If you want something, I get it for you. That's how I operate.

SUSAN: Nothing makes me sick.

MACK: He went across, sat down and ordered a meal.

COOLEY: Every time she came near the table I threw in a few quick quips to establish myself as a man of refinement and wit.

MACK: Such as: [*Imitating* COOLEY.] 'How about a roll or two?'
[*He chuckles in imitation of* COOLEY *chuckling at his own weak joke.*]

COOLEY: The secret is to wait for the right question. 'Where have you flown in from?' she says. 'South Africa,' I reply—there'd been a flight from Capetown unloading when I came through the gates.

MAL: South Africa. Why the hell would anyone want to say they came in from South fucking Africa?

COOLEY: I never mix politics and sex. It was just after that first rash of heart transplants. 'South Africa,' she said. 'Yes,' I said, 'I'm Adolf Voerward, Dr. Christian Barnard's anaesthetist and this, [*Indicating* MACK.] is my colleague Dr Villiers Van der Graf'.

KATH: [*looking at her watch and leaping up*] Oh the pizzas! Would anyone like some pizza?

MACK: Love some Kath, Cooley?

COOLEY: 'Well,' I said… yes thanks, Kath…

KATH: Simon, Jody? some pizza?

[*The others are less enthusiastic.* KATH *goes to the kitchen.*]

JODY: Did you manage to…?

[SIMON *glares at her.*]

MACK: Get into them?

[JODY *nods, but as if to say, 'That isn't quite how I'd put it'.*]
Cooley did, but my bird was biologically indisposed.

MAL: You've heard about the time I met the bastard in the Bistro?

[COOLEY *is very much aware of* KERRY *by this stage and aims his performance at her, without making it too obvious. He knows she is attracted by his consciously exaggerated male chauvinism.*]

COOLEY: There's no doubt about it. If you're after the straight fuck, no complications, that bistro is the best place in Melbourne. From Tuesday night onward you can't get in there for hard core twat. Medium to good quality secretarial stuff. [*To* KERRY.] Well, no sooner had Malcolm arrived than this great bird walked through. 'You want my body,' I said, 'don't you?' Which is a pretty standard approach of mine in those sort of circumstances.

[EVAN *has entered, bearing pizzas. He stands by* COOLEY'*s elbow.* COOLEY *notices him and breaks off.*]

KATH: If you'd like a bit of fresh air, take your food out onto the patio.

[*There is a drift to the patio.* EVAN *drags* KERRY *away from* COOLEY *and plonks her on the sofa.*]

KERRY: [*irritated by* EVAN] What's wrong?

EVAN: This party shits me.

KERRY: Do you want to go home?

EVAN: Do you?

KERRY: I promised I'd drop in and see Cam… I told you.

EVAN: You've been with him all the afternoon.

KERRY: We're working on his new environment. He needs me to check out the drawings.

EVAN: What! Are you doing his work for him now?

KERRY: Of course I'm not. He just hates sketching.

EVAN: It's about time you concentrated on your own work.

KERRY: What's that meant to mean?

EVAN: Maybe the critics had a point.

KERRY: You said you can't even understand the critics. Now you're trying to tell me they might be right.

EVAN: I can understand words like sloppy and self-indulgent.

[*Pause.*]

What time are you coming home?

KERRY: I thought we'd discussed all this.

EVAN: I'm not putting a curfew on you. I just want to know whether it's worth me staying up.

KERRY: I knew our marriage would be a disaster.

EVAN: [*stubbornly and loud*] It's not a disaster.

KERRY: Why don't you put a ball and chain on me? That's what you want, isn't it? Did you get my pizza?

EVAN: [*throwing the pizza on the floor*] There's your pizza.

[EVAN *storms out.* DON *approaches and sees the pizza on the floor.*]

DON: Troubles?

KERRY: Mmm.

DON: So's Whitlam.

KERRY: It's always my fault! I'm supposed to forego any meaningful involvement with anyone else but him!

DON: Oh.

KERRY: I'm seeing a lot of this marvellous sculptor. Not in the slightest bit remote. One of those naturally warm, vital people. You can see it in his work. Must have you and Kath meet him.

DON: [*flatly*] Great. What's his name?

KERRY: Cam.

DON: Cam White?

KERRY: His approach to the medium is very cerebral. In some ways

51

the philosophy is more important than the work itself and legitimately so. Evan caught us.

DON: I see.

KERRY: What Evan won't understand is that the growth of a relationship is organic. Sex is often a natural part of the growth. Deep down I think he concedes this, but he just can't stop himself acting out this compulsive male jealousy thing.

DON: Mmmm.

KERRY: It's so bloody immature.

> [*Pause.*]

Have you been writing anything lately?

DON: Still fiddling around. I got a poem published last week.

KERRY: Marvellous. Where?

DON: Newspaper.

KERRY: [*fake*] Marvellous.

DON: It was shit.

KERRY: Cam thinks it's hard to make words enigmatic enough to make them a viable artistic medium anymore.

DON: I don't know whether I'd agree with that.

KERRY: It's an interesting thought though, isn't it? You'll have to meet him.

DON: [*unenthusiastically*] Yeah.

> [COOLEY *has seen* EVAN *stalk out and thinks the time might be opportune.*]

COOLEY: [*to* KERRY] Hello, gorgeous. Care for a screw?

DON: [*to* KERRY] He used to say fuck.

KERRY: [*to* COOLEY] Any particular reason for the change?

COOLEY: I get more fucks when I say screw.

KERRY: [*to* DON] Is he always as blunt as this?

DON: Underneath there's a sensitive, vulnerable man.

KERRY: I don't believe it.

DON: He once fucked a woman with a tin leg out of sheer pity.

COOLEY: She was very well adjusted except that the knee cap squeaked.

KERRY: You would be one of the coarsest, most sex-obsessed persons I've ever met.

COOLEY: Actually, I'm a fine sexual technician.

KERRY: Who says?

COOLEY: I says. [*Under his breath, to* DON.] Piss off.

    [DON *goes, angry.*]

KERRY: You might be over-estimating yourself.

COOLEY: I might be.

KERRY: That's the first bit of modesty I've heard from you tonight.

COOLEY: I threw it in to intrigue you.

KERRY: I'm a little intrigued.

COOLEY: You're more than a little intrigued.

KERRY: Who says?

COOLEY: I says.

KERRY: How would you know?

COOLEY: I know a woman on heat when I see one.

KERRY: How?

COOLEY: Their eyes moisten.

KERRY: That's scarcely conclusive.

COOLEY: I have other tests.

KERRY: I have a husband.

COOLEY: He would be somewhere near Templestowe by now.

KERRY: I'm usually attracted to sensitive men.

COOLEY: Let's go before he gets back.

KERRY: Now?

COOLEY: Bloody oath. I'm flying back to Sydney tomorrow.

KERRY: It's very strange. This is the first time ever I've felt it would be right to go to bed with someone I've just met.

COOLEY: Crap.

KERRY: It's true.

COOLEY: Very flattering of you, my dear, but it's all crap.

KERRY: Usually it's an organic part of the whole relationship.

    [COOLEY *ushers* KERRY *towards the bedroom.*]

COOLEY: Organ first, relationship later.

KERRY: [*as she is going*] That's a very interesting philosophical proposition.

COOLEY: [*in the hall*] Let's discuss it further…

> [SIMON *looks at them going with disbelief and outrage.* DON *walks back inside munching a pizza. He looks for* KERRY *and* COOLEY, *realises what's happened and makes thumbing gestures in the direction of the bedroom—more, one suspects, in disgust at* KERRY *than at* COOLEY. KATH *comes up to him.*]

KATH: You might fill a few of those empty glasses.

DON: [*irritably*] They can fill them themselves. They've all got legs.

KATH: Jesus, you shit me. You're the one who throws these bloody parties and you won't even accept the responsibility of looking after your guests.

DON: Get stuffed!

> [*He storms out irritably to the kitchen and passes* SUSAN *on the way in.*]

SUSAN: Can I do anything?

KATH: There's nothing much to do.

SUSAN: Do you want me to collect the plates?

KATH: No. They'll bring them in.

> [*Pause.*]

Have you worked out some arrangement with my husband?

SUSAN: [*laughing nervously*] It's, er, not on.

KATH: Why not?

SUSAN: I suppose I was a little bit naive.

KATH: Yes.

SUSAN: In the circumstances. Do you often get strongly attracted to someone?

KATH: Not often.

SUSAN: I do. I don't quite know how to handle it.

KATH: So I've noticed.

SUSAN: The average man under thirty-five gets a sexual thought every five minutes. Did you know that?

KATH: No.

SUSAN: The average woman gets one every two hours. I think I must be oversexed.

KATH: Mmm.

SUSAN: When you think about it though, men are really inadequate. A turned-on woman could cope with ten men but I'd like to see the man who could cope with ten women. They're biologically inferior. Have you ever felt yourself strongly attracted to women?

KATH: [*backing off*] No.

SUSAN: There's nothing to be ashamed of if you have.

KATH: [*quickly*] I haven't.

SUSAN: I used to feel like that till I started going to encounter groups.

KATH: Encounter groups?

SUSAN: Group gropes. That's where I lost all my hang-ups. You ought to go on one.

KATH: [*relaxing somewhat*] Whenever I do get attracted to another man I get so guilt-ridden I run a mile.

SUSAN: Enrol in a group.

KATH: I really don't want to sleep with them.

SUSAN: [*musing*] Kerry's really beautiful, isn't she?

KATH: [*a little startled*] She's very attractive.

SUSAN: She's really beautiful. When I first saw her I wanted to go up to her and stroke her. A couple of months ago I would've felt guilty about that.

KATH: I think, er, Kerry's pretty conventional about sex. Prolific but conventional.

[EVAN *enters.*]

EVAN: Excuse me, Kath. Have you seen Kerry?

KATH: No. Isn't she outside?

EVAN: I couldn't see her.

[DON *enters.*]

KATH: Don. Have you seen Kerry?

[DON *shakes his head.*]

EVAN: No reflection on the party, Kath, but I think we might go home. I've, er, had a few late nights over the last couple of weeks and I think it's catching up with me.

KATH: I know the feeling. Don, have you seen Kerry?

DON: [*slightly irritated*] No, I haven't.

EVAN: She's not outside.

DON: Have you tried round the other side? She might be looking at my native trees.

> [EVAN *looks at him and moves out to the patio.*]

SUSAN: Shit. Where's Cooley?

KATH: [*accusingly, to* DON] Cooley's not with her, is he?

DON: I wouldn't know.

KATH: Don. You know what their marriage is like!

DON: What Cooley does is his own bloody business!

KATH: You might have warned him to lay off!

DON: [*lying*] I did.

KATH: I'm sorry Susan, but he's a bloody animal!

SUSAN: [*ruefully*]Yeah.

DON: [*to* KATH] What about Kerry!

SUSAN: If you think this is bad, you should have been at the last party. Ten minutes after we got there he had upset the hostess and had three of the men ready to toss him…

> [EVAN *strides through the kitchen again in the direction of the bedrooms. He looks grim and purposeful. The three in the kitchen look at each other. There is a ruckus offstage.* COOLEY *appears from the back half of the house with his shirt off and still struggling to zip up his fly. The noise continues in the background.* COOLEY *sees* DON *and indicates the bedrooms with his fingers.*]

COOLEY: Talk about coitus interruptus!

> [EVAN *strides into the living room and motions* COOLEY *with his thumb.*]

EVAN: All right! Get outside!

COOLEY: [*appealing to* DON] Call him off will you?!

EVAN: [*advancing on* COOLEY *and pushing him in the chest in the direction of the patio*] Get outside!

COOLEY: [*trying to maintain his decorum*] Look, fella. Be civilised! You don't go beating up people just because they take a liking to your wife.

EVAN: [*pushing again*] Get outside!

COOLEY: [*retreating*] Get outside. Get outside. What are you? A fucking parrot! I don't care what the circumstances are. You don't go interrupting a man and woman at their most intimate moment. What kind of a bourgeois shit are you?

KATH: Stop it!

> [KATH *is not heard or heeded in the din.* DON *is quite enjoying it. So are* MAL *and* MACK.]

EVAN: I'm going to hammer you, boy.

COOLEY: Keep your hands off me. I wouldn't like to be in your shoes if you catch me. I'll sue for assault. I'm a lawyer.

EVAN: I'll smash your teeth in.

DON: He's a dentist.

> [KERRY *walks in looking furious and dishevelled.*]

KERRY: Stop this at once!

EVAN: Get out of my way!

KERRY: You're acting like a bloody adolescent!

EVAN: You're acting like a bloody nymphomaniac!

KERRY: If you're not prepared to grant me some degree of emotional autonomy then that's it!

EVAN: Emotional autonomy? When you start screwing oafs like that it's emotional insanity!

COOLEY: Oafs! Look, boy. You can be as childish as you like but you just get your facts straight before you go calling people names!

EVAN: [*to* KERRY, *but looking at* COOLEY] Let's face it. When you start screwing boorish, load-mouthed oafs…

COOLEY: [*indicating* KERRY] What's so special about her, in any case? I've scored Miss Queen of the Pacific two years in a row!

EVAN: [*to* KERRY] Get your things!

KERRY: If you think this scene has given you some kind of moral leverage over me, you're wrong!

EVAN: Are you coming or aren't you?

KERRY: No. I'm not!

EVAN: I'll ask you once more!

KERRY: You can ask as many times as you like!

EVAN: [*turning on his heel*] Right!

KERRY: I'm not your personal chattel!

EVAN: And I'm taking steps to make sure I'm not yours!

KERRY: Are you threatening me?

EVAN: Work it out for yourself! Are you coming?

KERRY: No.

EVAN: I'll ask you once more.

KERRY: You can ask as many times as you like.

EVAN: All right if that's your final answer—that *is* your final answer?

KERRY: It is.

> [EVAN *leaves.* COOLEY *waits until he is out of earshot and bellows.*]

COOLEY: Don't show your face in here again, you shit!

> [*The guests look at* COOLEY *with looks ranging from disapproval to mild amusement.*]

END OF ACT ONE

ACT TWO

The guests are on the patio eating supper. MACK *wanders into the kitchen and turns up the* TV.

TV: … but the DLP support for Mr Joshua following a statewide trend of ten percent is expected to favour the Government. The importance of the DLP vote is again evident in the seat of Batman…

　　[COOLEY *wanders in from the fridge, bearing several cans.*]

COOLEY: Beer's holding out well. Party could kick on for hours yet.

MACK: Look at that bloody DLP vote.

COOLEY: [*holding up a can*] Do you want one?

　　[MACK *nods.* COOLEY *hands him a beer.*]

　　My old man voted DLP.

MACK: Yeah! I had an argument with him one day. Didn't like the permissive society. Wanted a return to Catholic moral purity.

COOLEY: He was the last of the great Catholic shaggers.

　　[COOLEY *turns down the* TV.]

　　He died on the job, you know.

　　[*Pause.*]

　　By the time they dressed him they couldn't put his teeth back in.

MACK: Yeah.

　　[*Pause.*]

COOLEY: Have you any of those photos on you?

MACK: What photos?

COOLEY: Of me and your wife.

MACK: What do you reckon? I carry them around in my wallet?

　　[*Pause.*]

COOLEY: Did they turn out all right?

MACK: A little under-exposed.

COOLEY: Did I photograph well?

MACK: Jesus, Cooley. I've just left my bloody wife.

COOLEY: Well it's a bit disconcerting for a man to know he has pornographic photographs of himself floating around.

MACK: They're selling very well.

COOLEY: Selling?

[*Pause.*]

What are they worth?

MACK: Five dollars for a set of six.

COOLEY: Save us a couple, will you?

MACK: Matt or gloss?

COOLEY: Matt.

[MACK *notes the order in his diary.* COOLEY *looks somewhat surprised at his efficiency.*]

MACK: Tell me something truthfully, Cooley.

COOLEY: Of course.

MACK: Ruth's an awful bitch, isn't she?

COOLEY: One of the awfulest.

MACK: It's not my imagination—she is a moody, temperamental, sour, irritable bitch.

COOLEY: She is definitely a moody, temperamental, sour, irritable bitch.

MACK: I've done the right thing leaving her?

COOLEY: You've done the right thing leaving her—I thought you were thrown out?

MACK: I left. [*After a pause.*] What's the scene like in Sydney?

COOLEY: So-so. Why?

MACK: I've got no particular reason to stay here.

[*Pause.*]

Will you answer something honestly?

COOLEY: What?

MACK: Am I a real kink?

COOLEY: Bloody oath.

MACK: Why do you think I did it?

COOLEY: Because you're a kink.

MACK: I think I was curious. She didn't respond to me so I wanted to see if she did with other men.

COOLEY: [*playing the good friend*] She didn't respond much to me.

MACK: Don't crap. I was in the bloody cupboard.

COOLEY: The trouble is you haven't had enough experience with women. Move in on that—what's her name?

MACK: Jody?

COOLEY: Mmm. She looks interested.

MACK: Her husband's here!

COOLEY: I'll get rid of him.

MACK: Do you really think she's interested?

COOLEY: Of course she is.

MACK: How will you get rid of him? Like you got rid of Evan?

COOLEY: Leave it to me. It's an art in which I have few peers.

[DON *and* MAL *wander into the kitchen.*]

DON: How's it going?

MACK: Fine if you're a Fascist.

MAL: Switch the bloody thing off.

[*Nobody does. Pause.*]

COOLEY: Well.

MAL: Well what?

COOLEY: I was just breaking a silence. Someone else can do it next time.

[*Pause.*]

MACK: Well.

COOLEY: Thank you.

MAL: Bloody intelligent conversation this is.

COOLEY: It's no use talking to you.

MAL: Why not?

COOLEY: You're in a shit because you've been swinging your dick at anything available and missing by yards.

MACK: As usual.

MAL: Shut your neck, you little gnome.

MACK: Can't face the truth.

MAL: You've never got onto anything but that bitch of a wife of yours in your whole life.

MACK: [*crushed but defiant*] Hah!

COOLEY: [*to* DON] And it's no use talking to you, either.

DON: Why not?

COOLEY: Something's happened to you.

DON: What?

COOLEY: Prematurely ossified brain or something.

DON: [*grinning, sending himself up*] You're referring to my new-found passion for native plants?

COOLEY: And slick brickies in high-density baby areas.

DON: [*still sending himself up*] You should see my mahogany gums. I got some nitrogen balls from the nurseryman.

COOLEY: Nitrogen balls?

DON: Yeah. Fifty-eight cents a half pound. They decompose over eighteen months and release nitrogen surreptitiously to the roots. Makes the neighbours think you've got green fingers. [*To them all.*] Do you want to have a look at them?

ALL: [*after a slight pause as they look at each other to decide whether he is joking*] No!

COOLEY: Time showed you two up, didn't it? [*Thinking.*] What is it… twelve, thirteen? When did I first meet the pair of you?

[*They muse and puzzle out the answer.*]

MAL: About fourteen years now.

COOLEY: About fourteen years. Some little prick was throwing a party.

MACK: Me.

COOLEY: I walked in the back door clutching my brown paper bag of bottles and watched in awe as Sutherland and Henderson, campus giants, womanisers, gave a virtuoso imitation of two men destined to leave their mark on the world. And now, fifteen years hence, I have to wince with embarrassment as I watch one of them trying to organise some third-rate extra-curricular sex with all the flair of a senile old bushwacker; and the other one being badgered into the suburbs by a bourgeois little *Home Beautiful* wife.

MAL: [*sarcastically,*] We're sorry we've disappointed you.

COOLEY: And I remember how grateful I was when you adopted me. Young Cooley. The little mouse. The grovelling, gaping, wide-eyed little boot licker. The boy who ran and bought the contraceptives. Young Cooley. Rescued from the Catholic choir. Fuck me! What did I have to be ashamed of?

MAL: He looks rather beautiful when he's angry, don't you think?

DON: The fluorescent catches the fiery glint in his eye.

MAL: You can see why we found him irresistible.

COOLEY: For five years of my life I let myself be patronised by a pair of posturing, self-inflated, bullshit artists.

DON: When were you ever patronised?

COOLEY: When? I was fucking easy prey. Don and his nympho nurse. Don's little Prefect with improvised lay-back seats. Anywhere. Anytime. Go on. Remember that?

DON: [*grinning*] I remember. I remember.

COOLEY: Little shit Cooley as he listens to big Don. [*Doing an imitation of himself.*] Eyes boggling. Hero-worship dribbling out of the corner of his mouth. And here's Don. [*Doing an imitation of a gruff-voiced DON.*] Ever stuffed a nympho Cools? Got one coming over tonight if you'd care to be in it. [*Imitating himself.*] Gee, Don. How do you know they are nymphos? [*Imitating DON.*] They just can't get enough of it, Grainger old cock. Anywhere. Anytime.

MACK: Was that the one he screwed in a traffic jam in St Kilda Road?

COOLEY: That story's another piece of Henderson crap!

DON: I didn't start it.

COOLEY: [*pointing to MAL*] No. Your mate here started that one. Very good mutual promotion between you two.

MAL: For Christ's sake. I just happened to make an offhand comment that she was so randy she'd be in it in a traffic holdup.

COOLEY: I spread it around for years. I made a legend out of the bastard—

DON: Some legend! I still run into people who look at me as if I'm some kind of insatiable sex fiend.

COOLEY: Not only the sex. The two great minds. [*Looking at* MAL.] Sutherland here plotting the right strategic moment to enter politics so that he'll make his way to the Prime Ministership with minimum delay.

MAL: Crap!

COOLEY: And Henderson carrying on lengthy debates on the relative merits of publishing in Britain or Australia first.

DON: It's a pity the bastard didn't go into politics. He's got a far better grasp of the complexities of the game than most of the clowns I've known who've got endorsements.

MAL: I wouldn't go along with that, Don, but I would go along with the fact that you've got talent and if you'd only pull your finger out, finish something and submit it for publication I'm sure you would get it accepted.

COOLEY: Here we go again. The way you two bastards lick each others' arses is really something.

MAL: [*irritated*] I'm not uncritical of the bastard. It's ridiculous that someone with his ability is teaching Fourth Form Social Studies in some tin pot high school at Doncaster.

DON: For Christ's sake let me fail in peace.

MAL: You don't get out of it that easily.

COOLEY: Neither do you, shithead. Australia's future Prime Minister. Protector of the exploited. Encyclopaedia salesman!

MAL: Christ, I only did it for a couple of months.

COOLEY: Eighteen, if I remember exactly. And correct me if I'm wrong, but didn't you make enough money in that time to quit working for two years and finish your course?

MAL: We lived pretty frugally.

COOLEY: [*doing an imitation of* MAL *delivering a monologue sometime in the past*] There's one point in the routine—and this is where it's really beautiful—when you've got them wanting those encyclopaedias so badly that you can toy with them. You can really get them scared that you are going to scoop up that great glossy lifesize photograph of the twenty-four leather-bound volumes and tell them the deal's off. I used to pause for a second and watch them quiver with desire for that great useless farrago of facts.

Then, very quietly, with a look of hurt doubt on my face, I'd say: 'Mr and Mrs Shitkicker—you don't really want the set, do you?' 'Yes,' they'd scream, 'stuff it in me kid. I want it. I want it. [*Taking an encyclopaedia from the bookcase.*] James Fygg 1695–1734 generally acknowledged as the first champion of England and fighting with bare fists, was born at Than, Oxfordshire. For years he was the leading pugilist and master of the noble art of self-defence. Stuff it in me kid. I want it.' 'Mr and Mrs Shitkicker, are you really enthusiastic, I mean really enthusiastic. Because, believe me, it is better to close the deal right here and now if you're not.' 'We are, we are,' they'd scream, and fear would redden the pupils of their eyes. [*Loudly.*] 'Then prove it. Come on. Prove it. Bounce up and down on your seats.' And there they'd be. The miserable, manipulated turds. Bouncing up and down on their seats for what they'd lose. Fuck all.

[COOLEY *resumes his normal voice.*]

I'm glad to see you here tonight cheering the People's Party, Sutherland.

MAL: Shit. You might try to take into account the circumstances. Jenny was pregnant again and—

COOLEY: Go on, you hypocritical bastard, you were as hungry for the dollar as the next man, Sutherland. Hungrier.

MAL: You must be joking.

COOLEY: Well, look at you now.

MAL: What do you mean?

COOLEY: You're making a fortune peddling bullshit.

DON: In all fairness I don't think lawyers are beyond reproach.

MAL: Beyond reproach is putting it mildly. The people that need lawyers the most can never fucking well afford them. Deny that.

COOLEY: I don't have to deny it. I'm not posing as the champion of the oppressed.

[*He walks out to the bathroom.*]

MAL: Bastard! At least I have a social conscience.

MACK: He just enjoys a good stir.

[*Silence.* SIMON *walks in.*]

SIMON: How are the elections going?

DON: It's not looking as good as it did earlier.

MACK: [*gloomily*] Postal votes always favour the Liberals.

DON: They've got more money to travel.

SIMON: Sometimes I don't think it matters much who wins. The country's run by the public service.

MAL: [*still simmering after his last encounter*] Don't be such a cretin! Broad policy decisions are crucial. Why do you think we've got the most miserable Social Service benefits, the worst schooling, damn near the worst health of any industrial nation?

SIMON: [*petulantly*] Why don't you go and live in Russia! [*He walks out to the patio.*]

MAL: [*looking at the others incredulously*] I'll hammer the cretin. I am going out there to hammer the cretin.
[*He follows him out. The women begin to re-enter from the patio.*]

DON: [*following him*] Lay off, Mal. I've had enough for tonight.

MAL: [*as he goes out*] 'Why don't you go and live in Russia!' He's got to be defective. Has to be. What is he? An accountant?

MACK: [*following them*] Probably a genius at mental arithmetic.

KATH: The way they carry on you'd think politics was right at the core of their lives. The most Don ever does in a practical way is hand out a few how-to-vote cards.

JENNY: Mal's just the same. He doesn't even hand out cards.

KATH: We'll just have to resign ourselves to the fact that we've married a pair of…

SUSAN: [*as* KATH *searches for the word*] Bullshit artists.
[*They laugh.*]

JODY: [*a little edgy at the treatment her husband is getting at their hands*] I think that there's nothing wrong with a discussion but I don't think people should argue with people they disagree with.

KATH: Don't worry about Simon. They're pretty harmless.

JODY: [*to* JENNY] How is Mal with your children?

JENNY: Very good. Why?

JODY: He seems to have quite a temper.

JENNY: The only pleasures in his life are oysters and political arguments. Don't begrudge him that.

JODY: I don't think it does his cause any good. It only antagonises people.

KATH: Talking about children. We're having terrible trouble with Richard at the moment. He just will not do anything we tell him to do.

JENNY: Oh that's the 'baulky' stage. What is he now? Three?

KATH: Just turned.

JENNY: Yes. They baulk at everything. It's in Spock.

KATH: Did yours...?

JENNY: Every one of them.

SUSAN: Don't let's talk babies. The men outside on politics, the women inside on babies. The all-Australian party.

JENNY: You wait till you have 'em. You'll prattle about them all the time.

SUSAN: I'm not having any.

> [*Pause.* JENNY *and* KATH *exchange glances.*]

JENNY: Well, that's your decision I suppose. Personally, for all the trouble they've given me, I wouldn't be without them.

SUSAN: I'm afraid they just don't turn me on.

JENNY: [*after another awkward pause*] How can you tell what your real feelings towards children are until you've had them yourself?

SUSAN: That's like saying you ought to eat shit in case it tastes like watermelon.

JENNY: [*tersely*] Having babies is not like eating shit!

SUSAN: I didn't mean it literally.

JENNY: Well, if you don't mind me saying so, it was rather a stupid comparison.

SUSAN: Look. If motherhood is all that wonderful why get so stirred up about anyone who looks like escaping it?

JENNY: Who's stirred up?

SUSAN: You are.

JENNY: I'm not stirred up. I just find it hard to argue with people who have no experience of life other than... sex.

KATH: Look, why don't we, er, change the subject? We've had one upset tonight already.

[*There is embarrassed silence.*]

KERRY: I must apologise about Evan.

KATH: [*taken aback*] Yes he, er, sounded pretty upset.

KERRY: Yes.

KATH: Do you think it's safe to go home for a while?

KERRY: Oh yes. He's always exploding for some reason or other.

KATH: You can stay here if you like.

KERRY: Thanks, Kath, but I've got somewhere to go.

JENNY: Why don't you leave him?

KERRY: [*taken aback by the directness*] Er, permanently?

JENNY: I don't know much about the background but one would gather that you're not at all interested in him.

KERRY: That's not true. It's just that there are aspects of other people that interest me as well.

JENNY: Have you got any children?

KERRY: No.

JENNY: I think it's wise to resolve things before you do.

KATH: [*tongue-in-cheek*] Jenny's got a bit of a headache.

KERRY: [*to* JENNY] Hasn't your husband ever been over-possessive?

KATH: I don't think that's Jenny's problem actually.

[JENNY *glares at* KATH, *who, quite enjoying things, pretends blithely not to notice.*]

SUSAN: [*to* JENNY] Don't you ever get strongly attracted to people?

JENNY: Yes, but I don't go—

[*She is going to say 'leaping into bed', but she is not willing to be quite that direct.*]

… doing anything about it.

SUSAN: Why not?

JENNY: Mal'd go off his head.

SUSAN: What about him? He's been trying to pick something up all night.

JENNY: Men are always trying to pick up something. It's in their makeup.

SUSAN: It's in our makeup too.

JENNY: Yes, but we can control it better.

> [*Pause.*]

What particular aspect of Cooley attracted you? Much as I like him he's the last person I'd—

SUSAN: [*defending* KERRY, *almost protective*] I can understand Kerry being attracted to him. A lot of women find him attractive.

JENNY: He must have hidden talents.

> [*There is a pause.* JODY *has been listening to the conversation with some fascination. She looks around tentatively.*]

JODY: Has he?

SUSAN: What?

JODY: Got...

> [*She searches for the words.*]

KATH: Yes. For Christ's sake what *is* Cooley like in bed? I've listened to ten years of suggestion. [*To* KERRY] What are the facts?

KERRY: Don't look at me. I didn't get a chance to form an opinion.

SUSAN: [*matter-of-fact*] He's not all that big, but he's inventive, durable and has quite a fair recovery.

> [*There is a pause as they digest the directness of this response.* KATH *feels a slight sense of liberation that she can talk about it.*]

KATH: Don plods on for hours. Bores me stupid.

SUSAN: The long slow grind. I didn't miss out on much.

KATH: What's Simon like, Jody?

JODY: Well he's not as big as my father...

SUSAN: Wow. That's progressive.

JODY: [*embarrassed but laughing*] I used to see him under the shower.

SUSAN: You can't always tell when they're in repose.

KERRY: I don't think size is all that important. I think it's much more important what type of communication exists on other levels.

SUSAN: Yes. I've known some fine little pricks in my time.

KERRY: [*looking at* SUSAN, *reproachfully but not angrily*] Seriously.

SUSAN: [*embarrassed and suddenly a little distracted under the gaze*] Yes. I was being facetious. People are more important than pricks.

KERRY: [*realising the impact she is having on* SUSAN] The most obvious proof of that is women being attracted to other women.

SUSAN: Mmm. That's right.

JODY: Does, er, much of it go on?

SUSAN: Oh yes.

JODY: Do they… er… lose interest in men?

SUSAN: Not necessarily.

JODY: It worries me a bit.

JENNY: It disgusts me.

SUSAN: [*to* JENNY] Why?

JENNY: The thought of touching another woman's body makes my flesh crawl.

KERRY: [*giving* SUSAN *encouragement that she never intends to follow up*] I think that the female body is infinitely more beautiful than the male.

SUSAN: That's right. Men are too square and knobbly.

JODY: How do women do it?

[*Pause.*]

SUSAN: Well. It all depends how…

[*She trails off as* SIMON *enters, puffs his pipe, and approaches the group.*]

SIMON: Don't, er, let me interrupt you. I've just come in to watch the television.

[*Pause.*]

Hmm. Has anyone seen *Exterminating Angel?*

SUSAN: [*nodding, as does* KERRY] Mmm.

SIMON: Do you find Bunuel's early work disturbing?

SUSAN: Mmm.

SIMON: Mmm. Very powerful. Very elliptic.

[*Embarrassed silence.*]

KERRY: Excuse me.

[*She moves towards the patio.*]

SUSAN: [*following her*] I think I'll see what's going on out there too.

[JENNY *follows them.*]

JODY: [to JENNY, *still irritated*] Where exactly do you live, if it's not being rude?

JENNY: [*cool*] We rent a house in Greensborough.

JODY: Are you going to buy?

JENNY: We're scarcely in a position to. We're four thousand dollars in debt.

KATH: Still?

JENNY: What do you mean still?

KATH: You've been four thousand dollars in debt for as long as I can remember. Mal's salary keeps on going up and up, but you're still four thousand dollars behind?

JENNY: Do you know how much Stephen cost us?

KATH: That was a long while ago.

JENNY: Over two thousand dollars!

JODY: Who's Stephen?

JENNY: Our eldest.

KATH: He was eight weeks premature.

JODY: Weren't you in medical benefits?

JENNY: [*curtly*] No, we weren't.

JODY: Why not?

JENNY: [*with heat*] Because by the time I found out I was three months pregnant, we weren't married and Mal was working as a base grade clerk.

[*There is an embarrassed pause.* DON *and* MACK *enter.*]

DON: [*cheerfully to* KATH] Can I turn up the television now?

KATH: What about a record? Something we can dance to.

DON: [*deviating obediently from his path to the television and going towards the stereo, still in a good mood*] Fair enough. I'll agree to anything. Mack, old cock, cast your eyes over all those ladies and select one. Simon. You too!

SIMON: [*going up to* KATH *as the music starts*] I'd like to have a dance with the hostess, if I may.

KATH: Thank you.

MACK: [*to* JODY] Have you had enough of me or will you chance it again?

JODY: [*dancing with him*] I don't like the sound of that.

DON: [*walking up cheerfully to* JENNY] Jenny?

JENNY: No thanks.

DON: Why not?

JENNY: I haven't danced for years.

DON: [*blustering, cheerful*] Well, it's time you did!

JENNY: I don't know any of the modern movements.

DON: So what? Neither do I.

> [DON *holds out his hands to indicate that she should get up and dance.*]

JENNY: I'd rather not!

DON: [*treating it as a matter of pride*] For Christ's sake get up and dance!

JENNY: Go away.

> [DON *stalks off to the other side of the room.* KATH *glares at* DON.]

DON: [*quietly, but angrily to* KATH] Well, fuck me! She sits there all evening with a face like Ghengis Khan! What am I supposed to do?

> [KATH *propels him in her direction. He goes, reluctantly.*]
> [*surly*] I'm sorry.
> [*Pause.*]
> For Christ's sake have a drink.

JENNY: I just get so depressed, Don.

DON: [*gentler*] Come on. You've got four beautiful children, your husband is second Lieutenant to God and still rising.

JENNY: [*bitterly*] Our marriage is a farce.

DON: So is mine.

JENNY: No, really. I'm just about going insane.

> [*Pause.*]
> I'd walk out if I had some place to go.

DON: You're an attractive woman.

JENNY: Yes. I can go up to a mirror any time I like, to say, 'Jenny, you are an attractive girl.' And I am, but I've got no guts. Let's face it. I've been out of the human race for ten bloody years.

DON: [*scratching his head*] Yes, well, er…

JENNY: Yeah. I know you're not the slightest bit interested but you can just sit there and listen.

DON: Yes, well, er…

JENNY: It's got so bad that we avoid each other around the house. How's that for a marriage, eh?

DON: Beats mine.

JENNY: We both love the kids. We make love too. Sick, isn't it?

DON: Separate.

JENNY: Mal can't afford to yet. When he does go I'll be a zapped-out fishwife and he'll be right on top of the shit heap and young enough to enjoy it.

DON: Have another drink.

JENNY: I've really lost it, Don. All I can do these days is sit in a corner and hate other people for their competence. I hated your wife for being a good hostess earlier tonight. That's sick, isn't it? It's getting so that the only people I can take are shits.

   [DON *reacts to the implication.*]

The thing that gets me—that bastard is climbing up out of it on my shoulders and I just have to stand there and watch him do it.

DON: Finish your degree.

JENNY: Stuff my degree.

DON: I just thought—

   [*He shrugs his shoulders.*]

JENNY: That's another thing that gets me about you lot. You crap on about a degree not being fit for anything but wiping your arse, but you'd cut off your balls for a Ph.D.

DON: I don't know what to suggest. Have an affair.

JENNY: You try having an affair after four kids have made your tits droop and your stomach look like someone's got stuck into a soggy steam pudding with a fucking whip. For God's sake—I've been trying for three bloody years. Knee touches under the table, haunting glances, I even got the plumber over the back to come and unblock the sink and all he said was, 'How's your kids?'

DON: Yeah, well that's—

JENNY: Let's face it. If you had to choose between me and that flat-stomached melon-breasted tart out there, who would it be?

DON: [*shrugging*] Well, it's all a matter of taste.

> [COOLEY *comes in from the patio. He notices* MACK *dancing with* JODY, *and looks across to* SIMON.]

COOLEY: Mack!

MACK: Yeah?

COOLEY: [*nudging* MACK *in the side, looking knowingly at* JODY] Getting on with it, I see. I think it's about time we swung into [*Pointing to* SIMON.] Plan Alpha.

> [*He gives* MACK *another drunken dig in the ribs.* MACK *shakes his head. The music stops.*]

This isn't the time for cold feet, m'boy!

JODY: [*not having seen the pointing to* SIMON, *etc.*] What's he talking about?

> [MACK *shrugs.* COOLEY *moves towards the main group.*]

KATH: [*to* SIMON] How's the cellar going, Simon?

SIMON: Well, I'm afraid the halcyon days of the good cheap red are gone.

COOLEY: That's for sure. A few years ago you could bottle a really good red for under forty cents a bottle.

SIMON: A little raw but with real potential. I remember I did a trip around the Barossa Valley back in sixty-three—

COOLEY: Sixty-three. My God what a coincidence.

SIMON: Were you over there in sixty-three?

COOLEY: Bloody oath. The old Barossa was really great in those days.

SIMON: There was a dignified old-world air about the whole venture. Unlimited tasting, a variety of cheeses to nibble. It's gone very commercial now, I'm afraid.

COOLEY: [*putting his arm around* SIMON's *shoulder*] I'm afraid you're right. Mind you my trip in sixty-three wasn't all roses. I got this stomach wog about halfway round the circuit and started shitting like a camel, actually, to be more accurate it was more of a dribble because I hadn't had anything but wine and cheese for days and the old sphincters didn't have anything solid to come to grips with.

Stung like a bastard but I was buggered if I was going to let any stomach wog get the better of me, so I stuffed a wad of newspaper down my daks and drove on. Did a quick change after each winery. I often pick up a stomach wog in South Australia. Do you have that sort of trouble over there?

SIMON: [*coolly*] No. Not really.

COOLEY: I really get uptight when some wog disrupts my biological rhythms. If I have a good solid shit at eight o'clock in the morning then the rest of the day falls into place. Do you shit at a regular time of the day, Simon?

SIMON: [*getting agitated*] Look do we have to—

COOLEY: What about you, Susy?

SUSAN: No.

SIMON: Do you really think excretion is an interesting topic of conversation?

COOLEY: Well, we all have to do it.

SIMON: Yes, but we don't have to talk about it.

COOLEY: What are you? An anal prude or something?

SIMON: I just don't enjoy talking about shitting.

COOLEY: You probably don't even enjoy shitting!

[*They laugh raucously.*]

SIMON: Excuse me Kath. It's getting pretty late. It's about time we went.

KATH: [*glaring at* COOLEY] Very glad you could come, Simon.

SIMON: [*walking over to* JODY] I think it's time we went, Jody.

JODY: [*protesting*] I'm just starting to feel relaxed.

COOLEY: What a pity. I wonder if there's some way we could arrange to get Jody home.

MACK: I could drive her.

SIMON: I'd rather you didn't.

MACK: Won't touch another drop.

COOLEY: No. I think Simon's right, Mack old cock. You're well over the legal limit. What about a taxi?

JODY: [*to* SIMON] That's a good idea. I'll get a taxi.

SIMON: I'd prefer it if you came with me.

JODY: You go home and get some sleep, dear. I'll get a taxi.

MACK: I can assure you, Simon, that I'm in a fit state to drive.

SIMON: Jody. I'd prefer it if you'd come with me.

JODY: Why?

SIMON: I just would.

JODY: Are you worried about me doing something?

SIMON: Of course I'm not.

JODY: Then go home and get some sleep.

SIMON: Will you get your things and come?

JODY: I'll come when I'm ready.

SIMON: What am I going to tell the babysitter when I come home without you?

JODY: Stuff the babysitter.

[SIMON *moves across to* KATH. KERRY *is speaking into the telephone.*]

SIMON: Well, er, thanks again, Kath. Jody's not very tired so, er, she'll stay a little while longer.

KATH: [*a little surprised*] Oh. Fine. I'm sorry about the, er…

SIMON: [*finally giving vent to his frustrations, doing up his coat with the buttons in the wrong holes, while speaking loudly so the others can hear*] I must say that I'm surprised that University educated people can be so bloody uncouth.

[*He leaves in high dudgeon.* COOLEY *thumbs him as he goes, winks at* MACK, *and goes to the bathroom.*]

KERRY: [*hanging up*] Thanks for the hospitality, Don.

DON: You're going?

KERRY: Mmm.

DON: I'll drive you.

KERRY: Thanks, but I've rung a taxi. How are things between you and Kath?

DON: Fine. Are you going home? [*As* KERRY *shakes her head.*] What are you going to do about Evan?

KERRY: What do you mean?

DON: He seems pretty upset.

KERRY: It's funny to hear you getting so worried about him.

DON: What do *you* mean?

KERRY: You were making a pretty determined effort to get me to bed yourself a year or two ago.

DON: That weakens my argument, doesn't it?

KERRY: It's just one of those unfortunate cases where one partner in a marriage develops and the other doesn't.

DON: Kerry, you have the one attribute shared by all great artists.

KERRY: What?

DON: Humility.

KERRY: [*flaring*] Yes. Well, I'm sick of being humble and I'm sick of that stubborn bloody stupid husband of mine hanging onto me like a leech—

DON: [*tapping her on the shoulder, cutting her off*] I'll get you a drink.

[*Out in the kitchen,* MAL *is trying to get* SUSAN *drunk.*]

SUSAN: Everywhere I go these days I put my foot in it.

MAL: [*still on the make*] Don't we all?

SUSAN: I try and be honest but you can't be. People have too many hang-ups. They hate you for it.

MAL: I know how you feel. People hate me for exactly the same reason.

SUSAN: No they don't. People hate you because you're a shit. Don't try and compare yourself to me.

MAL: [*putting his arm around her*] It's my defence mechanisms that are obnoxious. The real me is warm and gentle.

SUSAN: Yeah, well I've only noticed the mechanisms.

MAL: Pay that one. [*Chuckling.*] You know, I've got a real feeling that we hit it off.

SUSAN: [*surprised*] Us?

MAL: [*putting his arm around her*] Us.

SUSAN: You've got about as much sensitivity as a geriatric wombat.

[COOLEY *returns from the bathroom. He whispers in* KERRY's *ear and goes over to* SUSAN.]

COOLEY: You want to go, Susy?

SUSAN: Why? Do you?

COOLEY: [*peeling off banknotes*] I think I'll stick around a bit longer. You catch yourself a taxi and I'll meet you back at the motel.

SUSAN: I don't want to go back to the motel.

COOLEY: Why?

SUSAN: I want to stay.

COOLEY: You want to stay? Why do you want to stay?

SUSAN: Why do you?

COOLEY: [*looking at* MAL, *unbelieving*] Do you want to get off with him?

> [SUSAN *looks at* COOLEY *as if to say, 'What a thickheaded suggestion'.*]

MAL: Why shouldn't she?

COOLEY: Really?

SUSAN: No.

> [MAL *looks hurt. He goes off to sit by himself.*]

COOLEY: Well, who?

SUSAN: [*lying, as she wants to get off with* KERRY] No one.

COOLEY: [*handing her the money*] I'll meet you back at the motel.

SUSAN: [*snatching the money and preparing to leave*] I hope she spits in your eye, Cooley.

> [COOLEY *looks somewhat surprised at the vehemence of* SUSAN'*s reaction. A taxi horn toots outside.* KERRY *waves to* DON *and walks through towards the door. She pauses to speak to everyone left at the party.*]

KERRY: Well. It's been nice meeting you all.

COOLEY: [*surprised*] Hey. Just a minute.

KERRY: Got to run. Taxi's waiting. Thanks, Kath.

> [COOLEY *follows her out to the patio. He gives up the chase.* SUSAN *can't help grinning a little.*]

COOLEY: What are you laughing at?

MAL: [*sniggering*] Oh, how the mighty have fallen!

> [COOLEY *glares at* MAL, *goes up to* SUSAN, *grabs her arm and starts leading her to the bedrooms at the back. They are both drunk.*]

SUSAN: What do you think you're doing?

COOLEY: What d'you think I'm doing?

SUSAN: I'll tell you one thing. You're not doing what you think you're doing.

COOLEY: We'll talk about it in here.

SUSAN: You can just miss out on it for one night in your life. I'm not someone you can just leap on top of when there's nothing else around.

COOLEY: [*turning on charm*] Hey, listen. Baby. It's me. Cooley. Your old friend.

> [*The last of this is heard as they move offstage.* DON *wanders from the living room into the kitchen and watches the television.* MAL *is sitting on the stool.*]

MAL: Is it worth getting up to look at?

DON: [*shaking his head mournfully*] Frank McManus is singing 'When Irish Eyes Are Smiling'. Santamaria's just been granted honorary infallibility by the Pope and the Ghost of Dan Mannix has been seen shitting on Trades Hall.

MAL: [*forlornly*] I thought this was going to be an immoral party.

DON: Something didn't quite jell.

MAL: Everyone talks permissive but when it comes to the crunch—

DON: Yeah.

MAL: Put a hand on a woman's bum you get crippled. Isn't that just too middle class?

JODY: [*drowsily*] Shut your neck.

MAL: Well, look at you two. Itching to get into it but too gutless to try.

JODY: We're quite happy, thank you.

> [MACK *indicates the bedrooms with his head. He and* JODY *drift off.*]

MAL: [*mimicking*] We're quite happy, thank you. The hypocrisy rampant in this society is staggering.

DON: You don't have to tell me.

JENNY: What bullshit.

DON: It isn't bullshit.

KATH: You won't stop 'em now. They're into the mutual admiration stage.

JENNY: Twelve glasses?

> [KATH *nods.*]

MAL: Mindless people following mindless rules.

KATH: [*to* DON] Why don't you lick his arse?

DON: That's not very nice! I'm not ashamed of the fact that out of all the people I know Mal is one of the two worth listening to.

MAL: I've said exactly the same thing about you—[*Sharply.*] Who's the other one?

DON: Bob Hawke.

> [*Pause.*]

The trouble with you two is that you never question the social institutions around you.

MAL: Marriage, for instance. It would be very very difficult for man to conceive a more boring social institution than marriage.

JENNY: Boredom's not what's wrong with our marriage.

MAL: [*challenging her*] What is?

JENNY: The size of your prick.

> [MAL *is deflated.* KATH *is interested.*]

KATH: What's wrong with the size of his prick?

JENNY: Nothing. He's got an obsession about it.

DON: Still?

JENNY: Still.

MAL: [*wounded*] If you don't mind.

JENNY: Well, God Almighty—

MAL: If it's just an obsession then how come you never have an orgasm?

JENNY: How can I have an orgasm when I'm worrying about you worrying about the size of your member?

DON: Size has got bugger-all to do with it. Haven't you read the Yank research?

MAL: [*angry*] It's not small. I just think it is.

JENNY: And don't you bloody well deny that we spend half our waking hours worrying about money.

DON: Well, he makes a bloody sight more money than I do.

JENNY: [*roaring*] We happen to have four kids.

DON: [*drunkenly righteous*] Even so.

KATH: To be quite frank, Jenny, I can see why you're always in debt.

JENNY: I bet you can.

KATH: What's that meant to mean?

JENNY: Nothing, nothing. Carry on.

KATH: Let's face it. You are wildly—and I mean wildly—extravagant when it comes to spending on your kids.

JENNY: Is that so?

KATH: It's none of my business, but Don told me you spent over three hundred dollars on their Christmas presents.

JENNY: And who told Don?

MAL: I did.

KATH: That's insane.

MAL: She uses those kids as status symbols. Rip into the bitch.

JENNY: Well. If we're going to get personal just let me tell you that I think you are two of the tightest pair of bastards I know.

DON: [*offended*] Is that so?

MAL: For sure.

JENNY: It's none of my business but if you're going to make a big deal of inviting us all over you might feed us with something more substantial than chips and Twisties.

KATH: [*hurt*] What about the pizzas?

> [JENNY *picks up a bowl of Twisties and empties it behind the couch.*]

JENNY: Couldn't stand to look at them a minute longer.

KATH: Well. Now that we're making an issue of things, we weren't very impressed with your splendid party catering the week after we lent you the money.

DON: [*shaking his head*] Bloody thirty dozen oysters. I nearly choked on them.

MAL: You were always the one who admired my ability to live for the moment.

DON: That was before you started doing it on my money.

JENNY: For God's sake write them a cheque, Mal.

MAL: Right.

[MAL *whips a cheque book out of his pocket with a flourish.*]

DON: There's no need, I assure you.

[*Nevertheless he takes the cheque which* MAL *has just written.*]
[*surprised*] Two dollars?

MAL: That's all that's in there. Jenny's just bought a swimming pool for the kids.

KATH: A swimming pool?

JENNY: A swimming pool. I won't have my kids being patronised by that bloody cretin down the street.

MAL: A bloody plumber and he's got a fifty-by-twenty filtered pool.

DON: For God's sake, Jenny. A pool. Your whole life is centred around those bloody kids.

JENNY: What else can I centre it around? He gets me pregnant every eighteen months.

DON: [*to* MAL] Why in the hell do you get her pregnant every eighteen months?

MAL: She won't take the pill.

DON: [*to* JENNY] Why not?

JENNY: I get frigid.

DON: [*to* MAL] Use Silvertex.

MAL: [*with distaste*] Yuk!

DON: Withdraw.

MAL: I do.

DON: You do?

MAL: I make mistakes.

[*Pause.*]

Hey! Why do I make mistakes?

DON: Because you're a stupid prick!

[*He laughs uproariously.*]

MAL: Hey! I've just had a flash of insight.

DON: What?

MAL: Look. I've got hang-ups about my dick. Right.

DON: Right.

MAL: So I have dozens of kids as a symbol to prove myself. Right?

DON: Right.

MAL: The more kids I have the more money she [*Indicating* JENNY.] spends on them. Right?

DON: Right.

MAL: And the more worried we get about money, the harder it is for her to have orgasms, the more worried we get…

DON: You've finished!

MAL: Right.

DON: Right.

JENNY: Crap. You were worrying about the size of your prick long before we were broke.

MAL: Who's the bloody psychologist?

JENNY: Your mother said that the first words you ever said were 'widdle dicky'.

DON: How about some hypnotherapy?

MAL: Hypnotherapy?

DON: [*making the hand motions of a hypnotist*] Despite what you see in the mirror you have a big dick, big dick.

MAL: Very bloody funny.

[MAL *sees* JODY *standing in the hall. She's been there some time.*] What's happened to you?

JODY: Mack fell asleep.

[DON *and* MAL *laugh.*]

DON: He flaked.

MAL: Have a seat.

DON: We were just commenting on the size—

MAL: [*quickly stepping in, not realising that she has heard it all in any case*] The point that we were making is that everybody is hopelessly hung up about sex.

JODY: Including me.

MAL: Including especially you. Will you answer one question truthfully, Don?

DON: I might.

MAL: How are you and Kath hitting it off?

DON: Hah!

MAL: There you are. And we all know why.

DON: Why?

MAL: Boredom. Put a male and female rat in a cage and they'll go at it hammer and tongs until the male drops from exhaustion. Put a new female in and the male starts up again. What conclusion do you draw from that?

DON: He's a victim of the rat race.

MAL: I think you can all see from that little anecdote that it's sheer insanity not to swap wives.

JODY: My husband and I enjoy it.

MAL: What? Swapping?

JODY: No, doing it.

MAL: You had me worried! Now listen: it should be the most natural thing in the world for me to say to you, Don, 'Here, Don. Take Jenny for the night.'

DON: I don't think we could fit three in the bed.

MAL: It should be natural now, shouldn't it?

DON: Of course it should.

KATH: [*grimly*] It should. Should it?

DON: It should be the most natural thing in the world.

KATH: It's funny how you never have the guts to champion wife-swapping until you've had a gutful of beer.

MAL: Yes, I'm afraid that Don's greatest failing is his lack of moral courage.

DON: Is that so?

MAL: Look. I don't want you to take this as an insult, fella—and what I say I say as a friend—but you are a weak turd.

DON: [*loud*] I object to the use of the words weak and to a lesser extent turd.

MAL: Ten years ago it was all eyes on Don and watch Mal go down screaming, booted out of Uni. Tail between my legs. And what'd you all feel then, eh? I'll tell you what you felt. You felt, 'Serve you bloody well right, Mal'. And you weren't the only one: and the point I'm making is that I think I can feel justifiably proud of the way I dug my toes in and fought back. Let's not be modest. I fought back against bastards who were hoping that I was down and I'd stay down—and now—using economic criteria, which admittedly are very poor criteria to use—[*Yelling.*] I've shat on them. I've shat on the bastards and the bastard I've shat most on is Donald L. Henderson. I think you owe it to yourself to pull your finger out, boy.

DON: Now just a minute. Even when you were down I said: 'Mark my words. That man is down but not out. If any of us makes a million he will.'

MAL: I remember that. I remember that. I was very flattered.

DON: It wasn't meant as a compliment.

MAL: I know how you meant it.

DON: [*loud*] It was recognition of your talent for obsequiousness and bullshit.

MAL: You can. You can—[*Looking at his empty glass.*] get me another beer.

[DON *pours him a beer.*]

One thing about you two. I can always discuss issues of relevance here. [*In the manner of a great compliment.*] They are thinking people. [*To* DON.] We've had bloody great times.

DON: Remember Cooley's old man's pub?

MAL: Do I what?

DON: They were great days.

MAL: Bloody great days.

DON: Mal: I'd like you to have Kath for the night.

MAL: Don: I'd like you to have Jenny for the night.

[MAL *staggers drunkenly across the room to embrace* KATH. *She hits him with an efficient short jolt to the stomach. He crumples onto the carpet.*]

[*panting, winded*] I see.

DON: What are you doing down there?

[*He goes to help* MAL *up, but collapses on top of him. They laugh hysterically.*]

MAL: They were great days.

DON: Great days.

KATH: Oh, they were great days—great bloody days, weren't they? Then why the hell did I have to put you on an invalid's diet because you had ulcers at the age of twenty-five because you couldn't fucking well cope with your job or anything else for that matter and why did I have to cook all your meals and wash all your clothes? Eh? Because your little mummy hadn't told you that there's a fucking great world full of people out there who don't give a stuff about little Donnie Henderson, boy wonder, prematurely retired. Whizz kid. Adolescent genius, full grown bomb out. Fizzer. Squib.

DON: Family man, school teacher, gardener, tree surgeon, handyman, good provider...

KATH: [*undaunted*] I had to creep around our flat while Donnie Genius is tapping out his earth shattering novel that was going to place him, and I quote, 'amongst the ranks of the all time fucking greats'.

DON: I've never said that. That's a lie. I have never in my life even suggested that I have any more than a modicum of talent. I have never—

KATH: Delusions of grandeur weren't in the race! I had to wait seven fucking years before I was allowed to have a kid. Jesus Christ! I wasn't allowed to do pottery until last year because it was so mundane. You shit me, Henderson. You shit me completely. I'm going to bed.

[*She starts to go.*]

MAL: Look, Kath, I'd like to apologise.

KATH: [*turning on him*] You shit me even more.

MAL: [*whining*] What've I done?

KATH: You don't have to do anything, Sutherland. You're just a born shit.

JENNY: Leave him alone.

KATH: You shit me too.

JENNY: The feeling's mutual.

KATH: And make sure we get that other ninety-eight dollars by the end of the week.

JENNY: You're incredible.

KATH: Well, why shouldn't we get it? Your idiot of a husband's earning twice as much money as mine.

JENNY: Well, that just shows you what an idiot your husband must be.

KATH: I'm going to bed.

JENNY: So you keep saying.

[KATH *storms off.*]

MAL: [*to* DON, *still with drunken goodwill*] We mustn't let this quarrel affect our relationship.

DON: I swear I didn't say that I thought I was potentially one of the great novelists of our time.

MAL: You said it to me once.

DON: When?

MAL: In the Albion.

DON: [*emphatically*] I certainly didn't mean it.

KATH: [*off*] If you think our marriage is so bloody boring then get out, and take your kid with you.

MAL: [*indignant*] It's not my kid.

DON: She's talking to me, I think.

MAL: [*looking at* JODY] What are you laughing at?

JODY: Nothing.

MAL: [*as the thought strikes him*] Did you hear any of the stuff about my problem?

JENNY: [*laughing too*] For Christ's sake come home, stupid.

JODY: [*drunkenly, beckoning* MAL] C'mere.

[MAL *staggers across to* JODY.]

MAL: [*belligerently*] What?

JODY: I wasn't laughing about your little problem. I've got a little problem myself.

MAL: What?

JODY: Little breasts.

MAL: Really?

JODY: Really bad.

MAL: Yeah?

JODY: I go berserk with jealousy whenever Simon sees another woman's breasts.

MAL: That they are bigger than yours?

JODY: They're all bigger'n mine.

MAL: Breasts aren't important.

JODY: That's what I tell myself. Do you like bums?

MAL: Love bums.

JODY: Got a good bum.

MAL: Well there you are. Nature compensates. I've got a good head.

JODY: [*dubious*] D'you think so?

MAL: Do you really still have a good time with your husband?

JODY: Yes we—

MAL: Really?

JODY: It was getting stale for a while so we started doing it less often and we found the old zest came back.

MAL: I bet your husband thought of that.

JODY: It works.

MAL: [*nodding*] Let's see your tits.

JODY: No.

MAL: I'm interested.

JODY: Let's see your… problem.

MAL: No.

JODY: I'm interested.

MAL: Tell you what. We'll go down to the bedroom.

   [*They stagger off arm in arm.*]
Jody and I are going down to the bedroom.

JENNY: [*with forbearance*] You and Jody are going home.

JODY: [*to* MAL] When I first met you I thought you were really obnoxious.

MAL: People often make that mistake about me.

   [*They embrace passionately.* EVAN *strides in.*]

EVAN: [*grimly*] Where's Cooley?

DON: [*surprised*] Down in the back room.

> [EVAN *strides off resolutely.*]

Don't wake the baby.

> [DON *goes across to* JODY *and* MAL *who are embracing, and taps* MAL *on the shoulder.*]

Hey, Evan's come back.

MAL: [*stopping the embrace*] Really?

DON: Hmm. I think he's looking for Kerry.

MAL: Kerry's gone.

DON: [*pointing to the bedroom*] Be a good chap and go and tell him.

MAL: [*staggering off*] What do you want me to tell him?

DON: [*embracing* JODY, *who doesn't seem to mind the change of partner*] Kerry's gone.

> [MAL *staggers off.*]

MAL: [*yelling*] Jesus, I'm hungry. Hey Kath, how about some Cornflakes? You can afford a plate full of those, you mean bitch.

> [MACK *backs on, half conscious, pursued by* EVAN, *who is about to punch him.*]

MACK: It's me, *me*! I'm Mack.

EVAN: I'm sorry, Mack.

> [*He goes off to look for* COOLEY. MACK *staggers across to a bean chair and passes out.*]

MAL: Hey, lay off. Lay off, you mad bastard.

> [*A scuffle is heard.*]

EVAN: [*off*] Where's my wife?

COOLEY: [*off*] I have just about had enough of you.

MAL: [*off*] Kerry's gone.

EVAN: [*off*] Where?

MAL: [*off*] I haven't got a clue. I was just told to tell you. Jesus, I'm hungry. Are you hungry, Susan?

KATH: [*off*] Stop that noise. You've woken Richard.

EVAN: [*entering*] Don.

> [DON *breaks the embrace.* JODY *goes down to* MACK.]

DON: Oh, hello Evan.

EVAN: Has Kerry gone?

DON: I think she has.

EVAN: All right, Cam baby. Get ready for an assault on your artistic sensibility.

> [*The conversation is now overlapping and confused.* EVAN *storms out.* COOLEY *comes onstage looking disgruntled, nursing a bloody nose or a black eye.*]

DON: Looks like you took a hammering.

COOLEY: [*indignant*] Has he gone? He got me when I was putting on my daks.

KATH: [*off*] They've woken the baby.

SUSAN: [*off*] Isn't he gorgeous?

KATH: [*off*] I thought you didn't like babies.

SUSAN: [*off*] I like other people's.

COOLEY: This is the last party of yours I come to, Henderson.

KATH: Good!

COOLEY: If people can't settle their differences in a civilised way then it's pretty poor. Pretty bloody poor.

> [*He goes off to finish dressing.*]

MAL: [*reciting off the packet*] 'Extra G. High protein cereal with iron!' That's what I need. Iron in my soul and lead in my pencil. Every day your body uses protein to build and maintain healthy tissue, but your body can't store protein. Right, body! Here comes some protein.

JENNY: [*to* MAL] Come on. We're going home.

MAL: I'm ingesting protein.

> [SUSAN *appears.*]

SUSAN: [*to* DON] He looks a bit like you.

DON: [*to* JODY] I'll call you a taxi.

JENNY: We'll give Jody a lift home.

DON: Would you? That would be fine.

KATH: [*appearing*] Richard's upset.

DON: All right. I'll go and nurse him.

KATH: If you could cut the noise down it'd be a help.

JENNY: Sorry, Kath. I'm just trying to shift this oaf here.

MAL: Anyone else like some Extra G?

JENNY: [*pushing him towards door*] I'll give you some when we get home.

MAL: We've only got Weeties. I need the protein. Your body can't store it.

JENNY: Jody, are you coming?

JODY: Thanks for the party, Kath. Haven't enjoyed myself so much for years. I'm going to vote Labor next election.

MAL: [*to* JODY] You're a sweetie. A real sweetie.

[*They go out the door.*]

JENNY: Thanks, Kath.

KATH: See you, Jenny.

COOLEY: [*appearing with* SUSAN *in his grip*] Where's Mal?

[DON *points out the door.*]

[*taking* SUSAN *and leaving*] Mal!

SUSAN: Thanks, Kath.

COOLEY: [*off*] You saw it all. I might need you as a witness when I take that bastard to court.

DON: [*to* KATH] You go to Richard, will you? I'll just fix up Mack.

[*He throws a blanket over* MACK.]

MACK: [*momentarily recovering consciousness*] Great party!

DON: [*wearily*] Tremendous.

[*There is a banging at the window which makes him jump.*]

MAL: [*off*] See you later, Nabokov!

[MAL *chuckles loudly and raucously.* DON *grins and thumbs his voice. Silence.* DON *goes to the television set and turns up the sound.*]

TV: The Prime Minister, Mr Gorton, and the Country Party Leader, Mr McEwen, both claimed to have been returned to office with a narrow majority in today's Federal election. Mr Gorton claimed victory on the basis of sixty-three seats.

[DON *snaps off the television set. He takes out a packet of cigarettes but it is empty. He finds a butt in an ashtray, puts it in his mouth and flops down on the sofa. He lights a match.*]

MACK: [*raising his head*] Fucking great party.
> [DON *sits there a moment, ruefully. The match burns his finger.*
> *He flicks it out.*]

DON: Shit!

THE END

NOTES AND GLOSSARY

Some explanation on the preferential voting system may be useful
to the reader. The voter must place a number against every name
on the ballot paper, in order of preference. In the counting process,
the first count looks only to the first preference. If no candidate has
gained a majority, the votes given to the least successful candidate
are then distributed according to the second preferences indicated
on his papers. The process of elimination continues until one candidate has gained a majority of votes.

ASIO. The Australian Security Intelligence Organisation.

ALBION, The. A hotel in the inner Melbourne suburb of Carlton,
  quite close to Melbourne University and on the same block as
  the Pram Factory theatre.

AUSTRALIA PARTY, The. A small political party which origi-
  nated in 1966 as the Liberal Reform Group with opposition to
  Australia's military involvement in Vietnam as its central policy.
  In the 1969 elections it attempted to reach 'those independent
  minded voters throughout the country who were tired of the
  "machine" politics of the two main contenders for power, but
  who found themselves unable to accept the antics and aspirations
  of the DLP'.

BUNUEL, LUIS [b. 1900]. One of the grand, old men of European
  cinema. A Spanish film director consistently concerned with
  the unlovely aspects of the bourgeoisie. See *The Exterminating
  Angel.*

CAIRNS, KEVIN. Right-wing Liberal Party sitting member for
  Lilley in 1969, returned in the election.

DLP. The Democratic Labor Party, formed by anti-Communist ele-
  ments within the Labor Party in the 1950s. A numerically small
  political party, it nonetheless wielded considerable power in elections, thanks to the preferential voting system.

DONCASTER. A north-eastern suburb of Melbourne, about twenty kilometres from the city.

EXTERMINATING ANGEL, The [*El Angel Exterminador,* 1962]. A film of Luis Bunuel, dealing with a party at which the guests find themselves mysteriously unable to leave.

GAIR, VINCENT. The DLP leader and senator in 1969.

GORTON, JOHN GREY. Prime Minister of Australia and Liberal Party leader in 1969, returned in the election.

HAWKE, BOB. In 1969, the industrial advocate for the Australian Council of Trade Unions, to become president of the ACTU in January 1970; a Rhodes Scholar. Subsequently Prime Minister, 1983–91.

McEWEN, JOHN. Country Party leader and Deputy Prime Minister in 1969.

MACKAY, MALCOLM. Right-wing Liberal Party sitting member for Evans [NSW] in 1969, returned in the election.

McMANUS, FRANK. A senator prominent in the DLP.

MANNIX, DANIEL [1864–1963]. Roman Catholic Archbishop of Melbourne from 1917 until his death, an outspoken anti-Communist and DLP supporter.

SANTAMARIA, BARTHOLOMEW AUGUSTUS. Born in Melbourne in 1915, a leading spirit in the anti-Communist activity which led to the formation of the DLP in the 1950s. Not himself a member of the DLP, he ardently supported it in weekly **television broadcasts and in the activities of the National Civic Council, of which he was President.**

WHITLAM, GOUGH. Labor Party leader and leader of the Federal Opposition in 1969. Subsequently Prime Minister, 1972–75.

www.ingramcontent.com/pod-product-compliance
Lightning Source LLC
Chambersburg PA
CBHW041932090426
42744CB00017B/2022